Communications in Computer and Information Science   519

More information about this series at http://www.springer.com/series/7899

Christopher J. Headleand · William J. Teahan
Llyr Ap Cenydd (Eds.)

Artificial Life and Intelligent Agents

First International Symposium, ALIA 2014
Bangor, UK, November 5–6, 2014
Revised Selected Papers

Springer

Editors
Christopher J. Headleand
Bangor University
Bangor
UK

William J. Teahan
Bangor University
Bangor
UK

Llyr Ap Cenydd
Bangor University
Bangor
UK

ISSN 1865-0929   ISSN 1865-0937   (electronic)
Communications in Computer and Information Science
ISBN 978-3-319-18083-0   ISBN 978-3-319-18084-7   (eBook)
DOI 10.1007/978-3-319-18084-7

Library of Congress Control Number: 2015943056

Springer Cham Heidelberg New York Dordrecht London

Printed on acid-free paper

Springer International Publishing AG Switzerland is part of Springer Science+Business Media
(www.springer.com)

Preface

This volume contains the papers presented at ALIA2014: The First Artificial Life and Intelligent Agents symposium, held during November 5–6, 2014, at Bangor University, Wales.

ALIA was a two-day event, which invited specialists from academia and industry to discuss the latest research and challenges in this sub-field of artificial intelligence. Day 1 was opened by Prof. David Shepherd, Pro-Vice Chancellor of Research and Enterprise at Bangor University. This first day was research focused, with a series of chaired presentations, some of which were accepted for publication in this volume. The first day also included a keynote talk from Prof. Karl Tuyls on bio-inspired autonomous systems and robotics.

Day 2 involved various invited talks from the commercial sector, discussing current industry challenges in this field. This was chaired by HPC Wales in the morning, and New Computing Technologies (NCT) Wales in the afternoon. Both sessions involved workshops, allowing academia and industry to engage and interact.

The review process was undertaken in two stages. The first round of submissions was for presentation at the main conference. There were 20 submissions, 12 of which were accepted for presentation. The second round of submissions gave the authors of accepted papers time to respond to the reviewers' comments, and address any concerns raised during the presentation. From this round, the committee decided to accept ten papers for the proceedings.

The Organizing Committee would like to extend their thanks to Prof. Peter McBurney, of Kings College London, whose advice and recommendations during the planning of the event helped make the ALIA symposium a reality.

The ALIA symposium was sponsored by HPC Wales, the national supercomputing service provider. HPC Wales also helped secure grant support for day 2 via the Welsh Government's Collaborative Research and Innovation Support Program (CRISP).

March 2015   Christopher J. Headleand

Sponsor's Message

As part of a commitment to support the research objectives of the Welsh universities, we were pleased to partner with the organizers of the ALIA symposium to support the running of this event. In addition to sponsorship from ourselves, there was discretionary grant support via the Welsh Government's Collaborative Research & Innovation Support Program (CRISP).

Artificial life and intelligent agents is a highly interdisciplinary field of research, with applications in many areas including robotics, the creative sector, and life science. It is in a constant state of development and growth and can have a strong requirement for access to high-performance computing (HPC); therefore we were excited to be involved in this event.

HPC Wales is a company formed between the universities and the private sector in Wales, and provides integrated supercomputing services for businesses and researchers across Wales and beyond. Host to the UK's largest distributed general purpose supercomputing network, HPC Wales offers access to some of the most advanced computing technology in the world, along with high-level training and customized support to exploit it effectively.

HPC Wales' distributed supercomputing network has a 17,000-core, 320-Tflop capacity and is the third largest civil public sector facility in the UK. The network includes two large hubs in South Wales and further sites within Welsh universities and business centers.

Over the course of the venture to date, HPC Wales has supported the creation of nine new enterprises, over 140 new jobs, more than 420 products and processes, and induced over 3.7m of inward investment into Wales. The venture has provided training to over 2,000 individuals and helped to foster over 110 academic–industry collaborations.

March 2014   Laura M. Redfern

Organization

General Chair

Christopher J. Headleand   Bangor University, UK

Local Organizing Committee

Llyr Ap Cenydd	Bangor University, UK
Panagiotis Ritsos	Bangor University, UK
William J. Teahan	Bangor University, UK
Franck Vidal	Bangor University, UK

Session Chairs

Alastair Channon	Keele University, UK
Christopher J. Headleand	Bangor University, UK
Peter Lewis	Aston University, UK
William J. Teahan	Bangor University, UK

Industry Relations and Marketing Support

James Pack	High Performance Computing (HPC) Wales, UK
Laura Redfern	High Performance Computing (HPC) Wales, UK

Web Administration

Kieran Bold	Bangor University, UK
James Jackson	Bangor University, UK

Keynote Speaker

Karl Tuyls   University of Liverpool, UK

Program Committee

Llyr Ap Cenydd	Bangor University, UK
Tibor Bosse	VU University Amsterdam, The Netherlands
Stefano Cagnoni	University of Parma, Italy
Alastair Channon	Keele University, UK
Onofrio Gigliotta	University of Naples, Italy
The-Anh Han	Teesside University, UK

Christopher J. Headleand	Bangor University, UK
Benjamin Herd	King's College London, UK
Istvan Karsai	East Tennessee State University, USA
Ramachandra Kota	IBM Research, India
Tom Lenaerts	Université Libre de Bruxelles (ULB), Belgium
Peter Lewis	Aston University, UK
Johan Loeckx	Vrije Universiteit Brussel, Belgium
Jean Louchet	University of Ghent, Belgium
Evelyne Lutton	National Institute of Agronomic Research, France
Davide Marocco	Plymouth University, UK
Orazio Miglino	University of Naples, Italy
Simon Miles	King's College London, UK
Emma Norling	Manchester Metropolitan University, UK
Carlos Peña-Reyes	University of Applied Sciences and Arts Western Switzerland, Switzerland
Steven Phelps	University of Essex, UK
Gopal Ramchurn	University of Southampton, UK
Panagiotis Ritsos	Bangor University, UK
Elizabeth Sklar	University of Liverpool, UK
Tim Taylor	Monash University, USA
William J. Teahan	Bangor University, UK
Elio Tuci	Aberystwyth University, UK
Karl Tuyls	University of Liverpool, UK
Wiebe Van der Hoek	University of Liverpool, UK
Franck Vidal	Bangor University, UK
Peter Vrancx	Vrije Universiteit Brussel, Belgium
Peter Whigham	University of Otago, New Zealand
Payam Zahadat	University of Graz, Austria

Event Sponsors

ALIA2014 was sponsored by HPC Wales, host of the UK's largest distributed general purpose supercomputing network. Industry engagement was part funded by CRISP, the Welsh Government's Collaborative Research & Innovation Support Program.

Contents

Contents

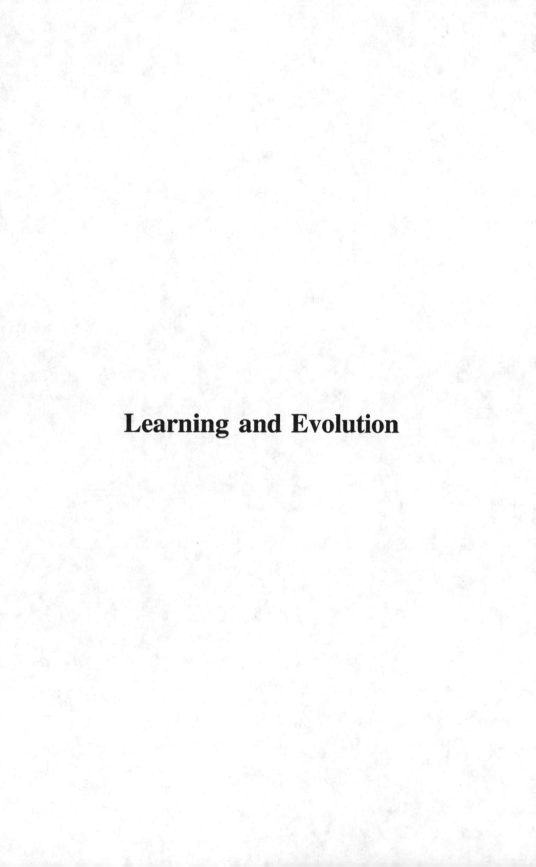

Learning and Evolution

Towards Real-Time Behavioral Evolution in Video Games

Christopher J. Headleand$^{(\boxtimes)}$, Gareth Henshall, Llyr Ap Cenydd, and William J. Teahan

Bangor University, Bangor, Gwynedd, UK
c.headleand@bangor.ac.uk

Abstract. This paper presents preliminary work in real-time behavioral evolution of non-player characters in video games. We present an approach, utilizing a modified version of the Template Based Evolution algorithm, to evolve NPCs during a first person shooter game. Through the research, we demonstrate how this approach could be a viable method of introducing evolutionary components into industry quality games, to produce procedural, emergent behaviors.

Keywords: Real-time behavioral evolution · Template Based Evolution · Games intelligence

1 Motivation

There are examples of using evolutionary algorithms in games, but these tend to be found in experimental, academic, or independent games, rather than high quality commercial developments. One of the possible reasons for this is that, while evolutionary algorithms have been used successfully to prime leading technologies, such as procedural animation systems, they can have turbulent effects in gameplay mechanics. There is no guarantee that they will evolve a solution that is engaging, enjoyable or consistent with the established design of the game. However, procedural generation in games is becoming a field which industry is beginning to pay more attention, partly because it can reduce development times on larger games, as every unique component need not be designed by hand, but also because it enables larger, open-world games where manual design may simply be impossible. It also introduces a new gameplay mechanic, by allowing the same player to have a different experience every time they enter the game world. Due to this interest from industry, evolutionary game content warrants additional research. We are interested in first person shooter games, where an individual's behavior is clearly observable, as we believe this is a particularly challenging domain.

2 Related Work

In the vast majority of modern, commercial computer games, all content (levels, characters etc.) is static within the game. This is almost always the product of

© Springer International Publishing Switzerland 2015
C.J. Headleand et al. (Eds.): ALIA 2014, CCIS 519, pp. 3–16, 2015.
DOI: 10.1007/978-3-319-18084-7_1

human, rather than algorithmic, design. This manual development is time consuming and expensive [1], with major titles often requiring hundreds of developers. Procedural content, when used, is generally limited to the randomization of a few start-up parameters. But even this needs to be tightly constrained to avoid generating undesirable content [2].

One of the few examples of commercial games that evolve content during play is Galactic Arms Race [3]. In Galactic Arms Race new content, specifically weapons systems, are evolved in real-time while the game is being played. To do this, the developers created the cgNEAT (content-generating NeuroEvolution of Augmenting Topologies) method, an extension of the NEAT algorithm [4]. The cgNEAT algorithm is used to evolve a neural network variant which genetically encodes particle system weapons. During the game, the weapons that the player use the most are monitored, creating a data set which is then used to evolve new weapons to suit the player's tastes [5]. This allows the player to ultimately determine how their game develops, and what content populates the scene. This has an added advantage of promoting replayability, and helping to ensure that players have unique experiences.

Another mainstream example of evolutionary content in a commercial game is Petalz [6] where flowers are procedurally evolved in an online game. It is designed, and implemented, as a social game on the Facebook applications platform, making it accessible to a large demographic of users. One of the principle objectives of the project was to assess the possible economic value of evolved content. In the game, users are encouraged to maintain and evolve a unique collection of flowers. Once they have created content, they can list it for sale on the virtual market place. This not only rewards the breeder, but also creates a form of collaboration, as once a flower has been bought, the buyer can create a whole new lineage. The results from the study indicate that the ability to buy and sell evolved content positively influenced the game dynamic, and facilitated social interaction. It also highlighted that user created content had value within the in-game economy [7].

One interesting game which developed out of research is Nero. In this game, the player evolves robots through training in a sandbox environment before deploying them against another player's team [8]. In this game, the evolution of the robots is integral to the gameplay mechanic, making it quite unique. Another interesting item to identify is that, similar to Galactic Arms Race, Nero uses a variation of the NEAT algorithm.

One study used evolutionary algorithms to train/optimize behavior trees for game bots in the commercial, real-time strategy game DEFCON [9]. The approach was capable of beating the Introversion bot (the bot which ships with the game) over 50 % of the time. In this research, each game represented a new evolutionary candidate, with fitness being calculated at the end of the match. This study highlighted the problem of using evolutionary algorithms for online learning in games, due to the time required to evolve a high fitness solution. Each experiment ran for 100 generations, and each generation had a population of 100 candidate solutions. With each game taking approximately 90 s to complete, four experiments would have taken 41 days of solid game play to complete the project. We also must assume that many of those candidates would have been poor quality solutions, and uninteresting to play against.

In another study [10], the concept of Ability versus Enjoyability is discussed, where enjoyability was defined (within the context of computer games) as the desire to play the game again after a match; in essence, the number of games the user will play before getting bored. The authors of this work hypothesize that optimal enjoyability is a function of ability; the AI controlled player should be hard to beat, but not too hard. Waiting 41 days (of continuous play) to produce a suitable solution may result in the player abandoning the game, something the authors refer to as a "shelf event".

There are also games where content is evolved offline, including the game environment [11] and the game play rules [12] but these are typically limited to academic projects. However, there are no examples of successful games where NPC (Non Player Character) behavior has been evolved in real-time. We believe that for real-time behavioral evolution to become a reality in commercial games, there are two concerns which must first be addressed:

1. If an evolved candidate is a poor solution, it must be removed from the game as quickly as possible, to prevent the player losing interest in the game due to poor gameplay.
2. Learning times must be reduced. A player is unlikely to wait for an interesting opponent to be evolved.

In the following sections, we will describe an approach which attempts to address these concerns.

3   Template Based Evolution

Template Based Evolution is a method for the behavioral evolution of virtual agents within a pre-designed set of constraints. Within this method, an agent's template is defined which contains all the possible inputs and outputs of the individual. These templates contain components to be evolved, including the traits of the agent, the conditions under which the inputs are evaluated, or the selection of an activated output (given a set of preconditions). By using this approach, a designer is able to define an agent prototype, and ensure that all evolved versions of this template still comply to a basic design criteria. This allows the designer to steer clear of problems that could be encountered if they had employed an open evolution method, such as invalid mutations, and implausible behavior.

Each TBE simulation is designed bottom-up, starting with the task environment and ending with the individual agents. The process is designed this way to force the designer to consider the ecological niche of the agents as the principle driver of evolution.

In the following sub sections we will provide a brief overview of the method. For a more in-depth description of TBE, see [13,14].

3.1   The Environment

The environment is the domain where agent fitness is tested through successive trials. A trial is a particular challenge that the agent must survive if they are to reproduce. These can be explicit obstacles such as a predator, or more implicit challenges, such as the need to migrate between two locations before a seasonal change [13].

TBE simulations make use of implicit fitness functions, which is the key purpose of the environmental trials. The key distinction between the two is that explicit fitness functions reward specific behavioral elements, shaping an overall behavior from a set of predefined primitives. Implicit functions, however, operate on a more abstracted level, rewarding the completion of a task, but the agent is free to complete it in any fashion.

3.2   The Species Template

The species template is a prototype of the agent being evolved. It contains a description of all the inputs and outputs accessible to each agent within that species, in the form of a subsumption architecture. A common code block is defined for each agent, with the agent's genome defining individual components within that block. From a game perspective, this has the advantage of keeping memory requirements low, as we only need to store an array of genomes rather than a variety of evolved phenotypes, which could be significantly more expensive.

3.3   The Agent

Each individual agent is defined by a genome, which is a collection of attributes. Each position in that genome has a specific role in structuring the behavior of the agent, or the conditions by which a layer of the subsumption architecture is either inhibited or suppressed. These positions are the same across all agents. For example, position 0 in the genome may define how every agent in the species processes an input, and position 2 may define the agent's speed. However, the values stored in each of these positions may be different in each agent, the product of their evolution.

The Genome in a TBE simulation is a collection of unique attributes, each attribute taking a specific role in the behavior of the agent. In the original paper [13], two attribute types were defined, trait and action. This was subsequently extended in [15] to include threshold attributes.

Trait. Trait attributes represent the 'qualities' of the agent, for example the color, speed or energy. They can be independent of the actual behavior of the agent (used outside the main subsumption architecture) but can also be used to modify specific behaviors; for example, a trait of speed may modify a run behavior.

Action. An action attribute represents an index value, selecting a specific action from an array of possible actions. As the agent traverses its subsumption, the output from each layer is determined by an action attribute. The actions available may be common across all layers, or alternatively, each layer may access a specific array of possible action.

Threshold. The third class of attribute described in [15] extended the possible applications of the method. This is used within a condition statement to define thresholds where layers may subsume or inhibit other layers. Additionally it may be used to define activation functions for input devices [14].

3.4 Modification for Real-Time Game Content Generation

Typically, as with most evolutionary algorithms, TBE uses a relatively large population and many generations. However, this would be inappropriate in a computer game where the player will combat against a limited number of agents, in a continuous fashion. As we established in the background to this work, traditional population, and generation sizes, may simply be inappropriate for gaming, due to the time taken to develop a suitable solution.

As discussed in the motivation, we are interested in first person shooter games. Specifically, we want to observe individual opponents (NPCs) that have the potential to exhibit unique combat styles. In our proof of concept game (described in the following section), the player will combat five agents successively during the game.

To modify TBE for this application, instead of evolving a new generation of agents to replace the previous, a new "brain" is evolved and deployed into the existing agents in the scene. If no existing agents are available (for example if the player has destroyed them) when a new brain is to be deployed, then a new agent is spawned at the edge of the environment to host it.

This cycle of generation, as opposed to being based on a set time or task, is instead triggered by combative engagements with the player. At the end of an engagement, the current genomes in play are evaluated and used to spawn the replacement genomes.

4 Proof of Concept Game

To test the use of TBE in real-time gaming, a test-bed, first person shooter (FPS) game was developed. In this implementation, a large game environment made of block obstacles is randomly spawned, with the player placed in the center. Then, five starting opponent NPCs are spawned at the edge of the map, in a position ensuring that they are initially occluded from the player (see Fig. 1).

The objective of the game is for the player to survive 5 min in the game world. The opponents have the ability to shoot the player, which is moderated for playability by an artificial stupidity function, which diminishes each opponent's accuracy at increased ranges. Both the player and the NPCs can shoot five rounds per second and survive 200 shots before being destroyed.

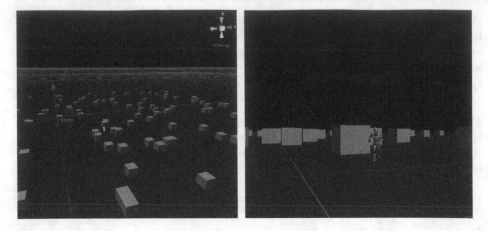

Fig. 1. A birds-eye, and player-perspective view demonstrating the randomly generated world. The player is spawned towards the center of the map, the team of opponents are spawned towards one of the edges.

When an NPC is destroyed, after a delay of five seconds, a new agent is deployed at the edge of the scene (the furthest edge from the player) to take its place, maintaining five NPCs in the game. The intention of the delay is to provide a short amount of time for the current combat engagement to conclude. The hope is that, when the new agent is spawned, it will be with a next generation brain. If no new brain is available, it would instead be spawned with the same brain as the agent who was destroyed (temporarily) until a new brain is available. The intention is to keep the game flowing for the player, ensuring a relatively consistent pace in the gameplay.

As each generation only contains five agents, a relatively high mutation chance and range is used to maintain diversity. For each attribute in the genome there was a 1 in 10 chance of mutation at each generation. The proof of concept game was developed in Unity3D [16] using the standard assets pack, and no custom assets were used in the game.

4.1 Species Template

The agent template is a subsumption architecture (see Fig. 2), activated by four inputs. The inputs allow the agent to know if it could see the player at different ranges, if it could hear one of its companions calling for help, and if it had been recently been shot (within 0.5 of a second). Each layer of the subsumption activated one of the seven behaviors described in Table 1.

The long-range vision length of the NPC was set to 50 units. For comparison, the width, height and depth of single blocks in Fig. 1 are equal to one unit. This gave them an equal long range vision to the player, who had their vision occluded (by fog) at 50 units. Short range vision was set to 15 units, as this represented half the range of the virtual firearms used in the game. The *Companion Heard* input had no maximum range, distress calls sent from the Call for Help function reached all NPCs in the scene.

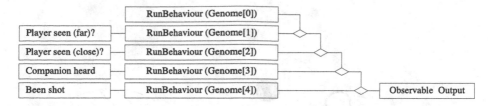

Fig. 2. A visual representation of the subsumption-based species template used within all the opponent agents.

Table 1. The actions available in the NPCs in the game, each action can be called from any of the 5 levels of the species template.

Shoot	If the opponent agent is able to see the player, and this behavior was activated, it would shoot in the direction of the player
Retreat	The agent would move in a direction 180 degrees away from the player
Run to NPC	The agent would move towards the direction of the last call for help. If there had been no call for help, then the agent would remain stationary
Call for help	The agent would call for help
Run to player	If the agent was able to see the player it would run towards it. If the agent was unable to see the player, it would move forward at its current heading
Explore	The agent would randomly explore the environment
Regroup	The agent would run towards the nearest companion agent

4.2 Evolution Cycle and Fitness

As mentioned in Sect. 3.4, the evolution cycle is defined not by a specific length of time, or the completion of a task, but is instead punctuated by the termination of an engagement with a player. An engagement is defined as a combat encounter between the player and one or more of the agents, notably that shots must have been fired, and hit at least one of the parties in the confrontation. The engagement is considered to have concluded when either the NPCs, or the player, have retreated outside the conflict zone, if no shots have been fired for 5 s, or if one of the engaging parties have been destroyed. Engagements are based on the player perspective, thus, if the player is engaged with one agent, and another joins mid-combat, it is considered a single engagement, not two separate engagements. The *conflict zone* is an area defined by the shooting ranges of the opposing NPCs participating in the engagement; this is illustrated in Fig. 3.

At the end of each encounter, the NPC rated the engagement in one of five categories:

Successful They inflicted more damage than they received.
Survived They received damage, but inflicted some.

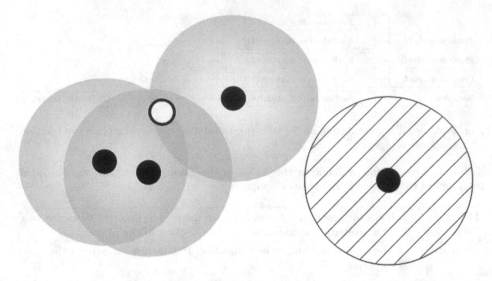

Fig. 3. A graphical representation of the conflict zone (gray). In this example, three NPCs (black spots) are engaged with a single player (white spot with black outline). The gray area created by the maximum ranges of their weapons is the current conflict zone. One NPC can be seen in the bottom right corner, though as it is not currently engaged with the player, its weapon range has not contributed to the conflict zone (indicated by a hashed radius, rather than a gray one (Color figure online)).

Retreat They received damage and inflicted none.
Destroyed The agent was killed in the engagement.
Inactive The agent took no part in the engagement.

If the agent is destroyed, it is removed from the gene pool and is unable to breed. Any remaining NPCs (post-engagement) are used to breed the next generation. Each breeding uses two parents to produce one child. The parents are selected randomly, but with agents that were marked as successful or survived being given a higher weighting (weighting of 2) to those marked with retreat or inactive (weighting of 1). This is with the intention of biasing towards proactive NPCs who engage with the player. This breeding cycle is repeated until five replacement brains have been generated.

If a single engagement results in all the NPCs being destroyed, leaving no parents, we still need a way to produce a new generation. In this case, we can assume that the NPCs have not evolved a tactic capable of competing with the player. If this happens, a new randomly created generation is spawned, essentially resetting the evolutionary process.

5   Pilot Study

In this preliminary study, 10 players each played five games (50 games in total), each game lasting five minutes (as described in Sect. 4). Each player was observed during the game, and their playing style was logged and categorized in one of four groupings, either aggressive, defensive, evasive or mixed (as described below). This logging was done on a per-game basis, assuming that players may change their style during the experiment. The investigator took a birds eye viewpoint, enabling them to observe both the player's, and the NPCs' behavior.

Aggressive. Aggressive players actively hunted opponents, searching the environment rapidly. Once they found the opponent NPCs, they would close the distance, engaging quickly.

Defensive. The defensive players tended to search not for opponents, but for easily defensible positions (areas with a large number of blocks creating cover). Once they had found a defensible position, they would stay close to it and use the cover to ambush NPCs where possible.

Evasive. Evasive players tried to approach and assault the enemy without being noticed using the blocks to hide when the opponent turned in their direction. If they felt that they had been spotted, they usually tried to flee, rather than continue the engagement.

Mixed. The mixed players employed a variety of tactics or no particular tactic during the game.

Additionally, during the game, notes about the NPCs' playing style were recorded for later analysis. The players were also asked to rate their enjoyment of the game on a 1 to 5 scale, and rate the "humanness" of the opponent they played against (also on a 1 to 5 scale). As a final data collection option, each player was given the option of a free text response, to allow them to record specific, qualitative data.

6 Results

During the pilot study, we made some general observations. We will discuss these before going into greater detail regarding player, and NPC specific observations.

Firstly, the evolving NPCs won around 2/3rds of the total games, 32 out of 50 (see Fig. 4). Initially we believed this to be quite high, an indication that the NPCs had evolved to be too competitive. However, we now believe this was simply a product of how the pilot study and proof of concept game were designed. Firstly, 7 out of the 10 participants lacked significant experience with FPS games, and were categorized as novice. Secondly, the users were not given a practice run, and all of their games were recorded. As a final point, while the NPCs had an unlimited number of 'lives' (a new opponent was spawned at the edge of the scene when one was destroyed), the player only had one, this greatly favored the NPC team.

However, even with these factors considered, we believe that the NPCs being able to evolve to compete with the player is still a significant result. The concept of NPCs having unlimited lives is also not an unusual concept in commercial games, and there is whole "horde mode" genera dedicated to it.

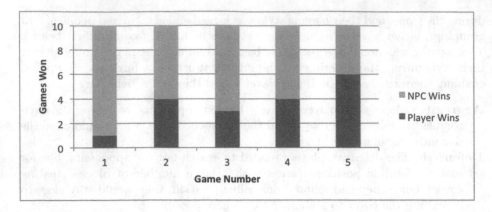

Fig. 4. Player and NPC wins over the 50 games. The NPCs were successful in approximately 2 out of 3 games, but players showed significant improvement in the final games.

6.1   Player Observations

Observing the player style produced some interesting data on how the players developed through the game (see Fig. 5). In the first game, players trended towards a mixed, naive style of playing as they learned to play the game and interpret the behavior of the NPCs. However, after the first game, 9 out of 10 players abandoned this style, and after three games, no player employed it.

After the mixed style of play, half of the players showed a preference towards an aggressive style (5 out of 10 players in games 2 and 3). After game 3, most players had opted to employ either a defensive, or evasive style, with the evasive accounting for 6 out of 10 players in game 5. This change in tactic seemed beneficial, as can be observed in Fig. 4. Although, one negative aspect of this playing style is that it prevented the opponents from learning a competitive strategy. Because the players would try to approach them without being detected, the engagements were often over before the NPCs had a chance to respond, rendering the evaluation mechanism moot. However, in the games where the NPC was successful, an interesting tactic emerged, which will be described in more detail in the following subsection.

While this observation is subjective, it does indicate that the players became quite reserved in actively engaging the NPCs. The two free text responses we had from players after game 5 seemed to support this, with one user stating "if you get too close to the opponent, they try to surround and ambush you". This anthropomorphism of the NPCs' behavior was not uncommon, and seemed to be tied into the player's enjoyment of the game. While the player's enjoyment of the game had little correlation to whether they won or lost, there was some correlation between enjoyment and the perceived 'humanness' of the opponent. This indicated that the anthropomorphization and believability of non-player characters may be important factors in the player's enjoyment of a game. This is further explored in the following subsection.

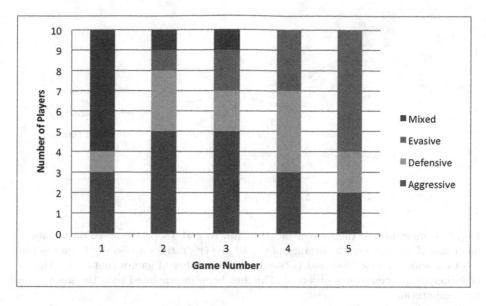

Fig. 5. Distribution of tactics employed by the players over the 50 games.

6.2 NPC Observations

While observing the NPCs, we attempted to categorize their behavior. The standard categories that we used for the players was not appropriate, as they only describe the behavior of a single agent, rather than a group. As we did not know what to expect between individual games and players, we chose to instead record when there appeared to be coordinated behavior between the NPCs. In these cases we logged "tactic observed" and attempted to describe the tactic seen. This data is presented and compared to the humanness assessment of the NPCs, and the player's enjoyment in Table 2 and Fig. 6.

In the earlier games (games 1 and 2), for all 10 players we noticed more coordinated behavior. We believe this was a product of increased player interaction, facilitating the evolutionary process. However, as the players moved towards more defensive, and evasive tactics, there was little to guide the evolution.

Table 2. Average player Enjoyment and Humanness assessment (0 to 5 scale), Tactics Observed are based on the number of games (out of 10) that coordinated movement of the NPCs was observed.

Game	Average Enjoyment	Average Humanness	Tactics Observed
1	3.7	2.7	6
2	4.1	3.6	8
3	3.1	2.2	4
4	2.7	2.4	5
5	2.3	1.5	2

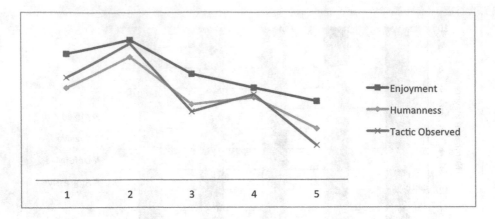

Fig. 6. Comparison of the Enjoyment, Humanness and Tactic Observed data. Enjoyment and Humanness are an average of the 10 player's ratings across the 10 games (on a 0 to 5 scale). Tactic Observed is based on the number of games (out of 10) that a coordinated movement was observed. This has been interpolated onto the same scale for comparison.

However, as we can observe in Fig. 6, there is a close correlation between the perceived 'humanness' of the NPCs and the games where tactics were observed. We can also see that this trend correlates loosely with the player's enjoyment of the game.

7   Conclusions

The game demonstrated that evolution can be applied to the real-time generation of behaviors. Moreover, those behaviors have, in some cases been perceived by the players as human-like, especially when the player employed tactics which promoted interaction. In the cases where the opponent was perceived as being more human-like, the player generally enjoyed the game more.

Another interesting insight we took from this is that when the player interacted with the NPCs, they trended towards learning roles within a team, rather than single agent strategies. For example, after one particular engagement, a team of NPCs were evolved who remained motionless, aside from a single agent who explored the environment and called for help when it saw the player, resembling scouting behavior. Another engagement produced a team of agents who confronted the player at different ranges (snipers and assault troops), keeping the player distracted. Tactics were evolved which allowed the NPCs to overpower the player roughly two out of three games, though losing the game had little correlation to the player's enjoyment.

One issue was that, if an NPC survived, its personality sometimes changed too drastically, breaking immersion in the game. One possible adaptation to solve this issue in future implementations would be to conduct a similarity match between the new genomes being deployed and the current genomes in play. The algorithm could then attempt to deploy new genomes to the host which has a similar current genome, causing a more subtle change in personality. Another option would be to only deploy new genomes when an agent is destroyed, or simply linearly interpolate between the old and new values.

This pilot study is limited in its conclusions due to the relatively small number of participants and games played. The next stage of this research will be to conduct a more in-depth user study to better assess the gameplay quality of evolved behaviors using TBE. Games developed in Unity3D can be deployed to a web page and played online. We are currently investigating the possibility of using this to reach a larger number of participants. Additionally, the next stage of this study will extend the template to allow for more complex behavior and add additional behaviors.

Acknowledgments. The authors would like to thank the reviewers for their insightful comments which helped guide the further development of the article. Additionally, Gareth Henshall and Chris Headleand would like to thank HPC Wales for the ongoing support of their research.

References

1. Irwin, M.: Game developers trade off (2008). http://www.forbes.com
2. Hastings, E.J., Guha, R.K., Stanley, K.O.: Demonstrating automatic content generation in the galactic arms race video game. In: AIIDE (2009)
3. Hastings, E.J., Guha, R.K., Stanley, K.O.: Evolving content in the galactic arms race video game. In: IEEE Symposium on Computational Intelligence and Games, 2009 CIG 2009. IEEE, pp. 241–248 (2009)
4. Stanley, K., Miikkulainen, R.: Evolving neural networks through augmenting topologies. Evol. Comput. 10(2), 99–127 (2002)
5. Hastings, E.J., Guha, R.K., Stanley, K.O.: Automatic content generation in the galactic arms race video game. IEEE Trans. Comput. Intell. AI Games 1(4), 245–263 (2009)
6. Risi, S., Lehman, J., DAmbrosio, D.B., Stanley, K.O.: Automatically categorizing procedurally generated content for collecting games. In: Proceedings of the Workshop on Procedural Content Generation in Games (PCG) at the 9th International Conference on the Foundations of Digital Games (FDG-2014). ACM, New York (2014)
7. Risi, S., Lehman, J., D'Ambrosio, D.B., Hall, R., Stanley, K.O.: Combining search-based procedural content generation and social gaming in the petalz video game. In: AIIDE (2012)
8. Stanley, K.O., Bryant, B.D., Miikkulainen, R.: Evolving neural network agents in the nero video game. In: Proceedings of the IEEE, pp. 182–189 (2005)
9. Lim, C.-U., Baumgarten, R., Colton, S.: Evolving behaviour trees for the commercial game DEFCON. In: Di Chio, C., Cagnoni, S., Cotta, C., Ebner, M., Ekárt, A., Esparcia-Alcazar, A.I., Goh, C.-K., Merelo, J.J., Neri, F., Preuß, M., Togelius, J., Yannakakis, G.N. (eds.) EvoApplicatons 2010, Part I. LNCS, vol. 6024, pp. 100–110. Springer, Heidelberg (2010)

10. Baumgarten, R., Colton, S., Morris, M.: Combining AI methods for learning bots in a real-time strategy game. Int. J. Comput. Games Tech., vol. 2009 (2008)
11. Togelius, J., De Nardi, R., Lucas, S.M.: Towards automatic personalised content creation for racing games. In: IEEE Symposium on Computational Intelligence and Games, 2007, CIG 2007, pp. 252–259. IEEE (2007)
12. Togelius, J., Schmidhuber, J.: An experiment in automatic game design. In: IEEE Symposium on Computational Intelligence and Games, 2008, CIG 2008, pp. 111–118. IEEE (2008)
13. Headleand, C., Teahan, W.J.: Template based evolution. In: Proceeding of the fifteenth annual conference companion on Genetic and evolutionary computation conference companion, pp. 1383–1390. ACM (2013)
14. Headleand, C., Ap Cynedd, L., Teahan, W.J.: Berry eaters: Learning colour concepts with template based evolution evaluation. In: ALIFE 2014: the Fourteenth Conference on the Synthesis and Simulation of Living Systems, vol. 14, pp. 473–480 (2014)
15. Headleand, C.: Bio-inspired methods for automatic behaviour generation. Master's thesis, Bangor University (2013)
16. Unity Technologies: Unity 3D (2004). http://unity3d.com/

Simulated Road Following Using Neuroevolution

Aparajit Narayan[✉], Elio Tuci, and Frédéric Labrosse

Aberystwyth University, LLandinam Building, Aberystwyth SY23 3DB, UK
{apn3,elt7,ffl}@aber.ac.uk

Abstract. This paper describes a methodology wherein genetic algorithms were used to evolve neural network controllers for application in automatic road driving. The simulated controllers were capable of dynamically varying the mixture of colour components in the input image to ensure the ability to perform well across the entire range of possible environments. During the evolution phase, they were evaluated in a set of environments carefully designed to encourage the development of flexible and general-purpose solutions. Successfully evolved controllers were capable of navigating simulated roads across challenging test environments, each with different geometric and colour distribution properties. These controllers proved to be more robust and adaptable compared to the previous work done using this evolutionary approach. This was due to their improved dynamic colour perception capabilities, as they were now able to demonstrate feature extraction in three (red, green and blue) colour channels.

Keywords: Road-following · Genetic algorithm · Neural network · Dynamic dimensionality reduction · Autonomous navigation · Active vision

1 Introduction

Autonomous navigation in its entirety is a vast and diverse field of study and research tends to be focussed on a number of sub-areas, such as steering control, obstacle avoidance, road-following, power management and road-sign detection. Amongst these, road-following or automatic driving on roads is an essential foundation of any system with desired autonomous navigation capabilities. While it may seem a trivial problem from a human perspective, accurately extracting the desired features in the environment and using them to navigate the road successfully is indeed a significant problem in terms of an AI system. This is particularly due to the amount of variance and non-uniformity present in terms of the geometry and colour composition of the road/non-road surfaces. Weather conditions such as rain, shadows, changing sunlight, etc., all have an effect on the systems visual perception of the environment and further complicate this problem.

© Springer International Publishing Switzerland 2015
C.J. Headleand et al. (Eds.): ALIA 2014, CCIS 519, pp. 17–30, 2015.
DOI: 10.1007/978-3-319-18084-7_2

1.1 Related Work

The design philosophy behind most engineered road-following solutions is based
on maintaining an internal model of the road/non-road environment which is
continuously updated based on the features extracted from the world [7]. A
commonly used technique is to use sensor fusion, combining sensory data from
multiple cameras and laser range-finders, to produce a more detailed and accurate representation of the world. This approach to the road following problem,
especially when adaptive techniques for maintaining the model of the environment are used has been successful in real-world trials. However at the core of
most such hand-crafted controllers is the issue of designer bias and the assumptions that are made of the road with regards to its geometry, contrast and colour
composition. Thus successful performance may be guaranteed in environments
accounted for in the design process, but often not across the entire range of possible scenarios such as in the case of [3] and [6] where geometric assumptions and
limited detail meant that the model was less suitable for more complex road-
shapes. There have indeed been a number of AI vehicles capable of complete
autonomous navigation over the years. The foremost of these in recent times is
Google's driver-less car project which logged over 500,000 km accident free during its road-testing phase. Others include Stanford's Stanley AI vehicle [8], which
won the 2005 DARPA grand-challenge after successfully completing a challenging
unstructured off-road course of 212 km. However in the case of such systems the
cost and hardware requirements often make their implementation prohibitive in
smaller low-power platforms. There have been a few attempts to use traditional
machine learning strategies to train neural networks to provide full navigation
control or at-least lateral steering control for autonomous vehicles, the foremost
among them being the ALVINN project [2]. The neural network employed was
a three layer feed-forward architecture with a single feedback unit. The input
layer was fed in readings from camera pixels and a laser range-finder. This initial road-following controller paved the way for the ALVINN-VC [7] which was
a more complete road-navigation system capable of dealing with junctions and
intersections.

One of the key challenges of the project was to provide data for the back-
propagation algorithm to train the network. In the case of road-following, training on the basis of real-world conditions to account for all the variations in
the road/non-road environment would be logistically impossible. Therefore great
effort was taken to create a simulated road-generator which would supply images
based on the variations of as many as 200 parameters. Later trials involved training the network on sensor and motor inputs generated by an actual human driver
in control. The main issue with the back-propagation approach to learning in
general is over-fitting to the training data and thus rendering the system less
effective in new un-encountered environments. Moreover there was still a level of
human bias manifesting in the choice and generation of the training environment
as well as the dictating of what the desired or perfect driving output of the controller should be. Such a control system, trained on human-driving data would
never be able outperform a human driving system and its best case scenario is

that of matching the human driving. It would also not account for unexpected scenarios such as the ability to recover from steering errors and deviations.

The evolutionary machine learning approach outlined in this paper attempts to provide an alternate solution to the road-following problem, one with minimal hardware/computational requirements yet with enough adaptivity to solve the entire range of road-following scenarios. It attempts at further reducing the dependency on human-foresight and allowing the AI control system to be in charge of learning its own feature extraction and control strategies. The authors of [1] who first implemented this approach, made use of a neural network with architecture similar to the one used in [2], but instead of supervised learning the authors used evolutionary computation. Apart from having outputs for controlling motor actions, the network had a further three outputs which were fed back to the input layer and were capable of influencing the perception of the input image. Instead of having separate modules for action and perception, the paper proposed a unified motor-sensory unit. This model bears similarity to the learning methodologies of biological organisms where functional behaviour is developed through interactions with the environment and a clear link is present between actions and their effect on the perception of the scene.

Thus the aim was to evolve a controller capable of road following behaviour with the ability to dynamically change its perception of the road as needed. Because of the prohibitive logistics of carrying out the learning on real-world platform, the evolution needed to take place in a simulated environment with the option of later transferring a successfully evolved controller to a real-world platform. As an initial proof of concept the experiment was successful in showing that such controllers can indeed be evolved to successfully carry out road following across a number of simulated environments. However there were limitations with regards to their dynamic colour perception abilities and as a result their performance in certain types of scenes which they had not experienced during evolution. This paper details further progress of solving the road-following problem in simulated environments using this active vision evolutionary robotics approach and aims at addressing the limitations of the previous methodology, techniques to ensure increased robustness and adaptability of the evolved neural networks, as well as further analysing and evaluating their behaviour. It is hypothesized that the strategies outlined in this paper would enable the evolution of controllers which would be capable of ultimately performing in real-world poorly delineated and unstructured roads.

2   Neural Network Controller

A Continuous Time Recurrent Neural Network (CTRNN) is used to control the robot as shown in Fig. 1. Eqs. 1, 2, and 3 define the activation values for the 25 input, 6 hidden and 7 output neurons. In these equations, y_i represents the cell-potential, τ_i the decay constant, g the gain factor, I_i the activation of the ith sensor neuron, w_{ji} the weight of synaptic connection from neuron j to neuron i, β_j the bias term and $\sigma(y_j + \beta_j)$ the firing rate. All input neurons share the same

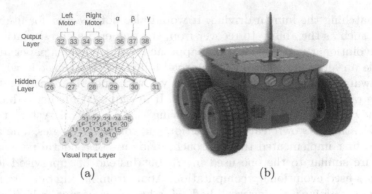

Fig. 1. (a) Architecture of the neural network controller. (b) The Pioneer robot.

bias (β^I); the same being true for output neurons (β^O). $\sigma(x) = (1 + e^{-x})^{-1}$ is the sigmoid function. The decay constants, bias terms, weights and gain factor are all genetically specified network parameters.

$$y_i = gI_i; \; i \in \{1, ., 25\} \tag{1}$$

$$\tau_i \dot{y}_i = -y_i + \sum_{j=1}^{j=31} \omega_{ji}\sigma(y_i + \beta_j); \; i \in \{26, ., 31\} \tag{2}$$

$$y_i = \sum_{j=26}^{j=31} \omega_{ji}\sigma(y_j + \beta_j); \; i \in \{32, ., 38\} \tag{3}$$

Due to the computational overheads associated with updating neural networks with large input layers, the number of input neurons was limited to 25. The image from the camera is divided into 25 equal-sized blocks. For each block, we compute the averaged red $(\bar{R})$, green $(\bar{G})$ and blue $(\bar{B})$ (i.e., average pixel value). Each block is associated with an input neuron and the final value I_i fed into an input neuron is computed in the following: $I_i = \alpha\bar{R} + \beta\bar{G} + \gamma\bar{B}$. The parameters α, β, and γ are generated by the network at each updating cycle, and normalised such that $\alpha + \beta + \gamma = 1$. These parameters give the system its dynamic dimensionality reduction properties. Each output neuron can increase or decrease the magnitude of these parameters to enhance or diminish the colour channel it is associated with, while at the same time having the opposite effect on the other two channels. For example, in an environment where red is the channel which shows contrast between road and non-road, having α at a maximum and the other channels at a minimum would enable the network to be presented with the best possible contrast from the scene. Figure 2 shows this effect of enhancing the correct colour channel to produce contrast between inputs corresponding to road and non-road areas.

The motion control is based on the 2D two-wheeled differential drive kinematics model for mobile robots detailed in [9]. This model takes into account the robots structural parameters i.e. radius, wheel distance and speed-limits to give an output in terms of the robots updated position and orientation. The output of neuron 32 to 35 (Fig. 1) are used to set the left and the right wheel speeds. Complex dynamical properties such as friction are not accounted for in this model. The author in [4] highlights examples of the successful portability of this model from simulated to real-world platforms.

3   Genetic Algorithm

A population size of 52 individual chromosomes is used, with a generational limit of 3000. Trials involved the network controllers trying to perform road-following in either six or twelve simulated environments. The best individual of each generation is guaranteed a place in the next generation, whereas the one which performed the worst is truncated and made unavailable for breeding. The rest 51 individuals of the new generation are generated by breeding with the parent chromosomes selected using the roulette-wheel method. Crossover and mutation probabilities are set at 50 % and 5 % respectively. These operators remain static and non-adaptive throughout the evolution. Carrying out this process of artificial evolution over 3000 generations in a sequential process would mean an unreasonably high training time. Thus the genetic algorithm is parallelized using MPI and implemented on the HPC Wales computing cluster. Each individual runs its evaluations as a separate process and the respective fitness values are communicated to a root process which in turn carries out the evolution, generating the new generation of controllers.

4   Simulation Scenes

The evaluation scenes are the virtual environment where each controller (i.e., chromosome) is evaluated. These scenes form the basis for the network's learning process, and the importance of this aspect needs to be stressed. These scenes have been designed to facilitate the evolution of dynamic colour perception strategies (i.e., the adaptive variation of α, β, and γ). The evolution scene graphics (see Fig. 2a) are rendered using OpenGL and are designed to simulate a camera pointing down at the ground such that the road and surroundings on either side are visible till a vanishing point further away.

The road is rendered using a modified version of the road generation algorithm employed in [1]. A total of 11 tiles are used each 160 cm long and 100 cm wide. The length of the road the robot needs to travel is 17.6 m. The virtual robot model has a diameter of approximately 54 cm. The road starts off with a smooth bend; each tile rotated 30° left or right. The direction of this turn alternates for consecutive trials. This is followed by a similar smooth bend, with greater probability (6/7) of it being in the opposite direction as the first one. This provision allows a controller to demonstrate the ability to make both kinds of turns and ensures the robot needs to be constantly maintaining its course to stay on the road. Subsequent turns are random, but checks are made to ensure no unrealistic or intersected road shapes are generated. The scene in each trial varies in

Table 1. Colour combinations of the twelve evaluation scenes.

Scene	Road	Non road	Random (Noise)
1	Bright Blue	Dark Blue	Red and Green
2	Bright Green	Dark Green	Blue and Red
3	Bright Red	Dark Red	Blue and Green
4	Bright Red, Dark Green	Dark Red, Bright Green	Blue
5	Bright Blue, Dark Red	Dark Blue, Bright Red	Green
6	Bright Green, Dark Blue	Dark Green, Bright Blue	Red
7	Dark Blue	Bright Blue	Red and Green
8	Dark Green	Bright Green	Blue and Red
9	Dark Red	Bright Red	Blue and Green
10	Dark Red, Bright Green	Bright Red, Dark Green	Blue
11	Dark Blue, Bright Red	Bright Blue, Dark Red	Green
12	Dark Green, Bright Blue	Bright Green, Dark Blue	Red

terms of the colour of the road and non-road surfaces as shown in Table 1. These scenes are created such that no contrast can be perceived between the road and non-road surfaces unless the robot is able to vary the value of α, β, and γ in an adaptive way. The 12 scenes can appear in three different formats, which differ in terms of the intensity difference between the dark and the bright colours (see Table 2).

To simulate the effect of poorly delineated roads, the edges of the textures were blended together such that there would not be a clear demarcating line between the road and non-road areas. It should be noted however that evolutionary runs carried out in roads without this effect (i.e. having a clear edge) did not demonstrate any behavioural difference. This can be attributed to the extremely low resolution of the final input image (25 pixels), which causes the network to be immune to such minor environmental variations. An additional road tile with higher levels of delineation and uneven geometry was created to be used in the testing period to assess the robustness of the evolved controllers.

Table 2. Contrast and colour distribution characteristics for the three sets of scenes.

Set	Contrast between mean intensities of road and non-road (0–255)	Range of distribution of intensities (0–255)
A	120 for all scenes	120 for all scenes
B	150 for mono-colour, 120 for dual-colour	10 for mono-colour, 30 for dual-colour
C	80 for all scenes	80 for all scenes

5 Road Bounds Checking and Fitness Function

Each trial is allowed a maximum of 250 iterations with a check being carried out after the end of each iteration (update) to see if the robot is still on the road. If the robot is detected to have moved off the road, the trial gets terminated. At the end of each trial the distance travelled is calculated by the number of road-tiles traversed thus far and the position in the current tile. In case of the trial being terminated due to the robot going off the road the current score value is divided by 5, to make the contribution of progress in the current tile negligible. This distance value $d(e)$ for each evaluation is further normalized to the range of 0.5–1.0 to present the final product, which would otherwise be a result of the powers of twelve or six, in an acceptable range. The final fitness function (Eq. 4) comprises of two components multiplied with each other, the product of distance values of each evaluation and the other a colour term Δ. In initial experiments, it was observed that the best individuals in the early stages of evolution were able to solve only a subset of the 12 scenes. These individuals dominated the population over generations, resulting in local maxima wherein the ability to solve the other scenes did not evolve. This happened in the case when the fitness was determined simply by the average distance value across all the trials. Thus having the fitness comprising of the individual distance values multiplied with each other ensures that such skewed solutions cannot dominate the population disproportionately and only individuals which perform consistently well in all the scenes are rewarded. Furthermore the Δ term was introduced to aid or guide the final solution by rewarding the correct activation of the colour outputs in each of the evaluation scenes. Populations initialized with the same random seed were tested in evolutionary runs with and without this colour term Δ to study its effect, and successful evolution was observed only in those runs where it was included.

$$F = \Delta_{final} \times \frac{1}{E} \prod_{e=1}^{E} (0.5 + (\frac{d(c)}{22})); \tag{4}$$

$$d(e) = NT + CS \tag{5}$$

$$CS = TL - \mu; \tag{6}$$

$$\Delta_{final} = \frac{1}{E} \sum_{t=1}^{t=E} C(e); \tag{7}$$

$$C_{1,2,3,7,8,9} = \sum_{s=50}^{s=S} |OR_s - OW_s^1| + |OR_s - OW_s^2| \tag{8}$$

$$C_{4,5,6,10,11,12} = \sum_{s=50}^{s=S} 2 \times OW_s \tag{9}$$

with $E = 12$ being the total number of trials; NT equal to the number of tiles crossed; CS equal to the score on the current tile; TL equal to the tile length; μ equal to the length of the error vector from the mid-point of the end of the

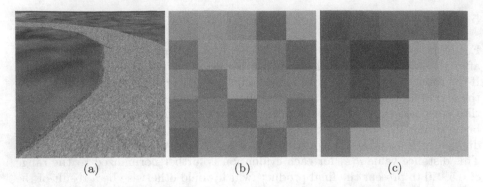

(a)   (b)   (c)

Fig. 2. (a) Grayscale image of scene 10 (see Table 1) (b) Pixel averaged version of the image with the three colour outputs (α, β and γ) equal. No contrast visible between road and non-road pixel grids. (c) Final pixel averaged version of the image with β activated, showing contrast between grids corresponding to the road and non-road areas (Color figure online).

road tile to the current position of the robot; $C(e)$ corresponding to the quality of the dynamic color perception strategy in trial e; OR_s being the value of the colour parameters (i.e., α, β, or γ) that has to be used to discriminate between road and non-road; OW_s^1 and OW_s^2 being the values of the colour parameters (i.e., a combination of α, β, and γ) that do not discriminate between road and non-road in mono-colour scenes; OW_s being the value of the colour parameter (i.e., α, β, or γ) that does not discriminate between road and non-road in the dual-colour scenes.

A final effect of Δ_{final} is that since it gets calculated only after the 50th iteration to allow the controller time to settle on a steady sequence of colour output values for the trial, any individuals leaving the road before the 50th iteration will get a 0 for the colour score of that trial. Thus those individuals which leave the road before the 50th iteration for all the trials receive 0 as the final fitness value irrespective of any distance values gained.

6   Results and Observations

The first round of evolutionary runs was done with six scenes. These constituted of three mono-colour (1, 2, 3) and three dual-colour (4, 5, 6) scenes. Scenes were created with textures chosen from Set A (see Sect. 4). Based on the results of this stage, the experiment was extended to all 12 scenes using textures from Sets A, B and C. Each experimental condition was tested with a set of 10 random seeds, resulting in a total of 40 evolutionary runs. Due to the nature of genetic algorithms and the complexity of the problem, not all experimental runs were able to evolve a successful solution. Only those experimental runs with fitness values high enough to indicate the ability to solve more than half of the evaluation scenes were selected for subsequent rounds of testing and evaluation.

6.1   Testing Round 1

In this first testing round the best individuals from the last 500 generations of eleven successful runs were subject to a uniform set of eight road shapes in each of the twelve scenes. The roads were generated to be approximately 24 m long. For each individual the inherent contrast levels in the scenes were the kept same as that they had experienced during evolution. The response of controllers to previously unseen lower contrast levels is discussed later in Sect. 6.2. The road shapes consisted of two basic types, an "S"shaped course where the robot needed to make turns in both directions to reach the end and the other where there was a constant turn in one direction followed by a straightening of the path. Each of these was generated twice with initial left and right turns for two different angles (20° and 30°) which dictated the curvature of these turns. During evolution the angle of curvature was always 30° and the road generation algorithm ensured that the overwhelming majority (6 out of 7) of shapes generated would be of the first "S" shaped type. The rationale behind generating this fixed set of road shapes was to discover the actual best performing individuals in the population. It was possible that some of the individuals which had obtained high fitness values could have simply been lucky and not possessed the ability to navigate multiple road shapes across all the environments. The re-evaluation tests also provided data on the performance of individuals in each of the twelve scenes, which gave an insight on the effectiveness and flexibility of their dynamic colour perception strategies.

A normalized distance score ranging from 0 to 10 was used to assess performance in each testing condition. Individuals that managed to reach the end of the road in a particular scene would thus get the highest possible score of 10. Figure 3 shows the average of this normalized distance score in each of the twelve scenes. Only data for solutions of evolutionary runs that used six scenes is included here. Figure 4 shows the same, but for solutions when twelve scenes were used during evolution. As during the evolutionary stage, the number of time steps (iterations) in each trial was fixed at 250. Thus individuals with higher scores not only demonstrated better strategies to stay within the road-boundaries but also greater speeds as they moved along the course.

Three out of the ten evolutionary runs using only six-scenes, provided solutions which could solve the three basic mono-colour scenes (road brighter than non-road) and all six dual-colour scenes (Fig. 3). This included scenes 10, 11 and 12 which they had not experienced during evolution. This is proof of the flexibility and adaptability of the solutions evolved. Not surprisingly they failed in the three reversed mono-colour scenes as the entire basis of their learning was dependent on the road being brighter than the non-road. On investigating the dynamic colour perception strategies of these controllers it was observed that the colour outputs for the three mono-colour scenes were more or less steady and above 0.85 throughout the trials. This was expected given their Δ values (see Sect. 5) from evolution being in the range of 1.4–1.8. However in places where sharp turns or course corrections were needed, a different behaviour

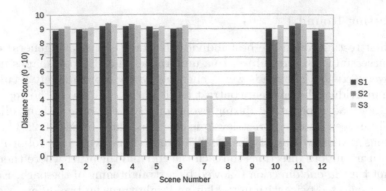

Fig. 3. Distance scores in the first round of testing for all twelve scenes. Shown in this graph are scores of the solutions of the three successful evolutionary runs using six scenes.

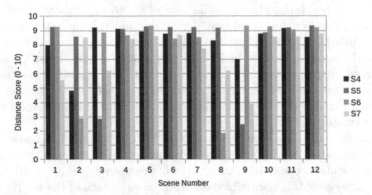

Fig. 4. Distance scores in the first round of testing for all twelve scenes. Shown in this graph are scores of the solutions of the four best evolutionary runs using twelve scenes.

was observed. The colour nodes instead of staying at a constant high value, oscillated between 0–0.9 every two time steps.

The inclusion of the mono colour scenes and the colour term (Δ) ensured that an adaptive strategy with utilization of all three colour output nodes was developed. It could be argued that including Δ in the fitness function was in a sense dictating a solution to the controllers, rather than truly allowing them to evolve their own strategy. However as seen from the results and during evolution it was indeed a necessary inclusion. Moreover the network did not completely adopt this enforced strategy as suggested by the presence of the periods of oscillatory behaviour displayed by the three colour outputs. It is interesting to note that the motion in terms of dynamics was smoother and faster when the correct colour output was constantly at a high value (≈ 0.9). During the oscillating phases the motion was slower and more uneven, with regular course-corrections having to be made.

The results of the twelve-scene experiments (Fig. 4) were not as uniform, with solutions showing greater variability in their colour perception strategies, depending on the seed and colour distribution set they were evolved in. The majority of solutions (like S5 and S6) only evolved the ability to dynamically vary two of their three colour outputs and simply did not use the third. This meant that two out of the six mono-colour scenes (basic and reversed) could not be solved. The unused colour output varied with each solution. However they did manage to solve all six dual-colour scenes because having the ability to dynamically vary only two colour outputs would be sufficient for these cases.

Only two solutions successfully evolved to show capability of solving all twelve scenes. Of these S4 evolved in scenes with colour distribution of Set B and S7 with distribution values of Set A. It is interesting to note the effect of these distribution values on the evolved solutions. The seed for S4 when used to evolve a solution with contrast values of Set A could develop only a sub-par solution where the controllers could not navigate the green mono-colour scenes. The seed for S7 when used with Set B, which could be said to be a less challenging environment, could only solve two scenes. Also unsurprisingly none of these seeds when tried with Set C could produce any solutions, as the contrast values were much lower and the distributions themselves were more spread out across the intensity spectrum.

Solution S7, developed a strategy wherein their ability to differentiate on the basis of the green channel was more enhanced than the other two channels. The β output was constant and near maximum for all scenes where bright green could be made the differentiating channel. For all other scenes, the colour outputs oscillated between high and low activations every third time step. While the controllers did traverse the entire course in scenes 1 and 2, the navigation was slower and often error-prone at the beginning, contributing to the lower average scores. Solution S4 evolved behaviour where the α, β and γ terms were near maximum for the majority of the time for scenes 3, 8 and 9 respectively. In the rest of the scenes it displayed periods of both stable and oscillatory activations of the colour output nodes.

6.2   Testing Round 2

Four individuals, two each from the two best six-scene and twelve-scene runs, were then chosen to be subject to a further round of testing. The aim of this round was to investigate the robustness and generality of their road-following strategies by observing their behaviour in environments they had not encountered during the evolutionary phase. The twelve scenes were recreated with textures having average contrast of 90 and deviations from mean of around 40 (on a scale of 0–255). In each of these scenes, the range of distribution of the random noise channels was set at 0–0.80 for one case and 0–0.25 in another. In the evolutionary runs, the distribution of the random noise channels always varied from 0–1 with uniform probability. However it was observed that narrowing this range to 0–0.5 during the testing phase caused a few randomly selected controllers to fail and thus it was decided to add this as a further evaluation parameter. In

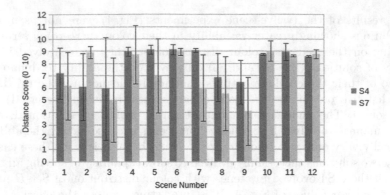

Fig. 5. Average scores received by the two best solutions in the second round of testing. The error bars depict the associated standard deviation values.

theory, controllers with the correct feature extraction strategy would be able to completely discard the random channels, as despite the range of the distribution it had no contribution towards highlighting the desired features. The road was set to be of the "S" shaped type with an angle of curvature of 25° in both left and right initial starting directions. These shapes were generated twice, giving a total of 4 trials for each random noise distribution value in each of the 12 scenes. Thus each individual in this second round of testing was evaluated for 96 trials. In order to further enhance the effect of presenting an unfamiliar environment to the controllers the road tile used in this testing phase represented a more delineated and unstructured course, having a maximum width of 110 cm at places but with only 85–90 cm consistently visible throughout. Figure 5 shows the distance scores of the two best solutions of this round, averaged across eight trials for each scene.

The results of this second round of testing (Fig. 5) showed that solutions S4 (twelve scenes) and S7 (twelve scenes) had developed the most robust and general-purpose solution. Despite receiving lower scores (below 7) for a few scenes, only these solutions had the capability of solving all twelve scenes across all the evaluation parameters, i.e. all road shapes with reduced contrast and varying random noise values. The performance of S1 (six scenes) in identifying features in the blue or γ channel was affected by the reduced contrast in the colour distribution. This in turn not only meant failure in the corresponding mono-colour scenes but also in the two dual-colour scenes where the blue channel was brighter on the road. The other two channels could still be successfully used across both ranges of the random noise variation. It was later tested in a scene with average contrast for the blue channel at 109 (still a new environment), and in this case it was able to navigate the corresponding scenes successfully.

While the solution S2 was able to solve almost all scenes when the random noise was in the range of 0–0.80, it failed to differentiate on the basis of both blue and green channels when this range was reduced to 0–0.25. This resulted in lower average scores for scenes 1, 2, 6 and 12. The inability to perform in these scenes was because it incorrectly associated the low distribution range of random values in the red channel with the availability of features. Thus it could see no contrast between the road and non-road surfaces in those scenes where red was not a feature differentiating channel.

For the two successful solutions in this round, it can be seen that in both cases performance in all but one mono-colour scene deteriorated compared to the earlier round of testing. They were still capable of reaching the end of the road in these scenes, but with less consistency compared to the earlier tests contributing to the lower overall score. Interestingly despite being subject to higher contrasts than S7 during evolution, S4 was still able to match or exceed its performance in eleven out of twelve scenes. On observing the behaviour of the controllers in these lower contrast scenes, it was seen that there was a disparity in their sensitivity to the three colour channels. For each solution there was a particular colour channel in which the ability to perceive contrast was much more pronounced. The controllers changed their colour perception strategies in these scenes, relying increasingly on oscillating the activations of the colour output neurons. However when the channel they were most sensitive to was available, they used it exclusively by activating only the associated output neuron for the majority of the trial.

7   Conclusions

The methodology described in this paper was successful in evolving neural networks capable of demonstrating road-following by dynamic dimensionality reduction in a variety of challenging simulated environments. This new set of controllers have shown improvement in the dynamic colour perceptions abilities compared to those evolved earlier in [1], with the capability to now recognize features based on negative and positive contrast in all three primary colour channels used. These improved results were brought about by the careful design of simulation scenes as well as the formulation of the new fitness function incorporating the colour-term Δ. This work is a significant step towards the hardware implementation of these controllers, as real-world environments would in majority consist of colour combinations similar to those present in the simulated scenes. However it is acknowledged that the contrasts between road and non-road surfaces would be lower than what the networks were tested on. This is proposed to be mitigated by introducing a simple contrast stretching step before the processing of the inputs. Future work would also focus on representing the environment in terms of alternate colour models such as HSV, instead of the traditional RGB model used thus far. Besides this, there is a need to increase the robustness of these controllers by minimizing the disparity in the feature extraction capabilities across the three channels. On the whole however, the findings of this paper strengthen the potential of using these controllers as a viable alternative road-following solution and further efforts would focus on transferring these evolved controllers to a mobile robotic platform.

References

1. Clarke, S., Labrosse, F., Trianni, V., Tuci, E.: An evolutionary approach to road following: a simulated case study. In: 12th European Conference on Artificial Life, pp. 1017–1024. MIT Press, Taormina (2013)
2. Pomerleau, D.: Neural network vision for robot driving. In: Hebert, M.H., Thorpe, C., Stentz, A. (eds.) Intelligent Unmanned Ground Vehicles, vol. 388, pp. 1–22. Springer, US (1997)
3. Sotelo, M., Rodriguez, F., Magdalena, L., Bergassa, L., Boquete, L.: A color vision-based lane tracking system for autonomous driving on unmarked roads. Auton. Robots **16**(1), 95–116 (2004)
4. Clarke, S.: Thesis: An Evolutionary Approach to Road Following. Aberystwyth University, Aberystwyth (2012)
5. Ososinski, M., Labrosse, F.: Real-time autonomous colour-based following of ill-defined roads. In: Herrmann, G., Studley, M., Pearson, M., Conn, A., Melhuish, C., Witkowski, M., Kim, J.-H., Vadakkepat, P. (eds.) TAROS-FIRA 2012. LNCS, vol. 7429, pp. 366–376. Springer, Heidelberg (2012)
6. Ramström, O., Christensen, H.: A method for following of unmarked roads. In: IEEE Intelligent Vehicles Symposium Proceedings. IEEE (2005)
7. Pomerleau, D.A., Thorpe, C.E.: Vision-based neural network road and intersection detection and traversal. In: Proceedings of the International Conference on Intelligent Robots and Systems, vol. 3, pp. 3344. IEEE (1995)
8. Montemerlo, M., Thrun, S., Dahlkamp, H., Stavens, D.: Winning the DARPA grand challenge with an AI robot. In: Proceedings of the AAAI National Conference on Artificial Intelligence, pp. 17–20. AAAI Press (2006)
9. Dudek, G., Jenkin, M.: Computational Principles of Mobile Robotics. Cambridge University Press, Cambridge (2000). ISBN 0521568765

Enhancing Active Vision System Categorization Capability Through Uniform Local Binary Patterns

Olalekan Lanihun[✉], Bernie Tiddeman, Elio Tuci, and Patricia Shaw

Department of Computer Science, Aberystwyth University, Aberystwyth
SY23 3DB, UK
oal@aber.ac.uk
http://www.aber.ac.uk

Abstract. Previous research in Neuro-Evolution controlled Active Vision Systems has shown its potential to solve various shape categorization and discrimination problems. However, minimal investigation has been done in using this kind of evolved system in solving more complex vision problems. This is partly due to variability in lighting conditions, reflection, shadowing etc., which may be inherent to these kinds of problems. It could also be due to the fact that building an evolved system for these kinds of problems may be too computationally expensive. We present an Active Vision System controlled Neural Network trained by a Genetic Algorithm that can autonomously scan through an image pre-processed by Uniform Local Binary Patterns [8]. We demonstrate the ability of this system to categorize more complex images taken from the camera of a Humanoid (iCub) robot. Preliminary investigation results show that the proposed Uniform Local Binary Pattern [8] method performed better than the gray-scale averaging method of [1] in the categorization tasks. This approach provides a framework that could be used for further research in using this kind of system for more complex image problems.

Keywords: Categorization · Active vision system · Neural network · Genetic algorithm · Uniform local binary patterns

1 Introduction

Active vision is the process of exploring a visual scene in order to obtain relevant features for subsequent meaningful and intelligent processing. This is very important and very useful in that visual systems usually have a form of control, and are intelligently guided to only those areas of the image surface being processed that have relevant and valuable information to the task at hand. The control of the visual system can be done by various techniques, although it is natural to use a Neural Network because of its biologically based inspiration and also their suitability for noisy data. However, developing an Active Vision

© Springer International Publishing Switzerland 2015
C.J. Headleand et al. (Eds.): ALIA 2014, CCIS 519, pp. 31–43, 2015.
DOI: 10.1007/978-3-319-18084-7_3

System, particularly using the approach of a evolving Neural Network is still in its elementary stage [5]. In most cases only simple vision problems have been solved using this approach, which could be attributed to inherent illumination conditions such as reflection and shadowing in natural images, and also the computational cost that generally comes with using evolutionary techniques for more complex image problems. As a result, when the problem domain becomes more complex, the dimension of the feature vector input to the network increases, and therefore the benefits from this kind of system are soon outweighed by the computational cost. Consequently, categorization using active vision has been used for more simple vision problems and discrimination of very few stimuli. For instance in [1], an Active Vision System based Genetic Algorithm evolved Neural Network was used for categorizing five gray-scale italic letters. In [5], an Active Vision System Genetic Algorithm evolved neural controller was used for basic 2D shape discrimination. In an attempt to overcome these problems, we have used Uniform Local Binary Patterns [8] for feature extraction and enhancement of more complex images taken from a Humanoid (iCub) robot camera. This can filter out to an appreciable degree impacts of image lighting conditions such as reflection and shadowing.

2   Related Works

The field of Evolved Active Vision Systems for categorization has been extensively studied. Mirolli et al. [1] used an Active Vision System that is based on a Genetic Algorithm evolved Neural Network to categorize gray-scale italic alphabet letters in different scales (sizes). The movement of the artificial eye was controlled by motor neurons of the output units, which determine the eye location per time step, in-order to capture relevant input features for the neural controller. James and Tucker [5], developed an Active Vision System that is able to discriminate different 2D shapes by moving about in any direction with an ability to zoom and rotate. The system was able to discriminate different 2D shapes irrespective of their scales, locations and orientations. An Active Vision System controlled by an evolved Recurrent Neural Network was developed by Morimoto and Ikegami [6] which dynamically discriminates between rectangular and triangular objects. In this system when the agent moves through the environment it develops neural states which are not just a symbolic representation of rectangles or triangles, but allow it to distinguish these objects. In the same vein Aditya and Nakul [2], used a Neuro-Evolution based Active Vision System to discriminate a target shape. The artificial retina used in their system has the ability to translate in co-ordinate X and Y directions, zoom-in and zoom-out, and ability to rotate as it scans over the image features. However in their work, they introduced constraints to the environment of the active vision based system. The constraints to the environment are implemented in the form of force field in a certain direction. At each time step during the training and evaluation, a unit force is exerted on the artificial agent by the force field. This implies that at each step, the agent is forced to move a unit direction in the direction of the force field. Consequently, the actual movement of the agent per time step is determined by the vector sum of the change of location in X and Y directions as well as the force movement. The constraints were added in order to make the system closer to the real world and also provides an opportunity to observe if the system is able to develop intelligent strategies for coping with them. In all the experiments, the system performed better in the discriminating tasks, despite the constraints introduced. Floreano et al. [3], also implemented an active vision based system that autonomously scans through gray-scale images and was able to discriminate triangular shapes from square shapes. The images used in their experiment varied in scale and location. Finally, in relation to other research works listed above, the approach in this paper also uses an Active Vision System based on Genetic Algorithm controlled Neural Network. We have adopted a similar approach used by Mirolli and Nolfi [1], but extended with the enhancement of the images with Uniform Local Binary Patterns [8] to categorize more complex images from a Humanoid robot's camera.

3   Experimental Details

We have used a biologically inspired Active Vision System that combines sensorimotor information in order to control an artificial agent. The artificial agent is provided with a moving eye that explores a visual scene (image), in order to extract relevant information and process the sensory stimuli. The vision system is controlled by a Recurrent Neural Network evolved by a Genetic Algorithm, which is similar in approach to [1]. We have adopted the same fitness function used by Mirolli et al. [1], but with a slightly different Recurrent Neural Network architecture, of similar update equations to [7]. We have also adopted the periphery only architecture of [1] (Fig. 1), which gave the best results in all the different architectures used in their experiments. We shall refer to the entire eye region as the periphery in the remainder of this paper. We have performed three sets of experiments, which are: (i) the replication of the periphery only architecture of the original Active Vision System experiment presented in [1] for the categorization of five italic letters that is, (l, u, n, o, j), which uses the gray-scale averaging of the pixel values of the periphery region; (ii) our proposed method of pre-processing the periphery region with Uniform Local Binary Patterns [8] for the categorization of the objects on more complex images taken from the iCub camera, namely: soft toy, tv remote control set, microphone, board wiper, and hammer; (iii) the periphery only architecture, using gray-scale averaging of the pixel values, but in this case it is used to categorize the same set of objects of images taken from the iCub camera. The neural network, evolutionary process and the fitness function are the same for the three experiments, except that in Experiment Two we have a different input vector size as the visual features are being processed by Uniform Local Binary Patterns [8]. The number of trials and generations in Experiments Two and Three are 250 and 5000, while that of Experiment One are 50 and 3000. In each experiment we evaluated the performance of the system based on its ability to correctly label the

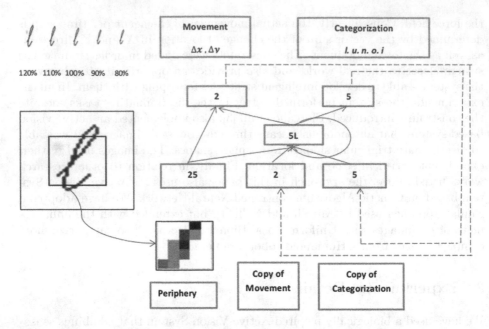

Fig. 1. The architecture of our adopted periphery only network used in Experiment One. It has 32 input neurons, 25 of which are for the periphery visual stimuli and 7 for efferent copies of the movement and categorization units. It also has 5 hidden neurons and 7 output neurons (that is, 2 for movement and 5 for categorization units). The left side of the figure shows the different variations of the letter l, and the periphery vision scanning part of the letter with white image background (Color figure online).

category of the letters or the objects. The three experiments were undertaken for quantitative and qualitative comparisons.

The Neural Network. The Neural Network is a recurrent architecture that consists of one input layer. The visual input vector size is determined by the method chosen for visual feature processing. It is 243 in the case of Uniform Local Binary Patterns [8] and 32 for the gray-scale averaging method. It also has one hidden layer of 5 recurrent neurons, and an output layer of 7 neurons. In the output layer, 2 of the neurons determine the movement of the eye per time step (maximal displacement of $[-12, 12]$ pixels in X and Y directions), and the other 5 neurons are for labelling the category (letters in Experiment One, and objects in Experiment Two and Three). The input layer consists of units which encode the current state of activations of the neurons for the visual stimuli of the periphery region, the efferent copies of the 2 motor neurons, and the 5 categorization units at previous time step $t - 1$. The activations of the input neurons are normalized between 0 and 1, and a random value with a uniform distribution within the range of $[-0.05, 0.05]$ is added to those of the gray-scale methods at each time step, in order to take into account the fact that the gray level measured by the photo-receptors of the periphery is subject to noise. The outputs of the neurons in the hidden layer depend on the input received from the input neurons through the weighted connections and the activations of the hidden neurons at the previous time step. The input activations scaled by the gain factor are represented by equation (1) below;

$$y_i = gI_i; i = 1, ., k; \tag{1}$$

where k stands for the size of the input vector, I is a vector of activation values of the inputs, y_i is the activation value of an input scaled by the gain factor g. The update equation for the hidden neurons is as shown in equation (2) below;

$$\tau_i \partial y_i = -y_i + \sum_{j=1}^{n} w_{ji} \sigma(y_j + \beta_j); i = 1, ., 5; \tag{2}$$

the update equation (2) for the hidden neurons is a differential equation. τ_i is the decay constant, y_i is the output of a hidden neuron at previous time step $t - 1$, n is the total number of the input and the hidden neurons, w_{ji} is the weight of a connection from an input neuron to a hidden neuron, $\sigma(y_j + \beta_j)$ is the firing rate (where β_j stands for the bias terms). Equation (3) below is used to compute the output activations;

$$y_i = \sum_{j=1}^{5} w_{ji} \sigma(y_j + \beta_j); i = 1, ., 7; \tag{3}$$

where y_i is the activations of an output neuron, w_{ji} is the connection weight from a hidden unit to an output unit, σ is the sigmoid function used as shown equation (4);

$$\sigma(c) = \frac{1}{(1 + e^{-c})} \tag{4}$$

The Evolutionary Task. In each trial the eye is left to freely explore the image, however, a trial is terminated when the eye can no longer perceive any part of the letter or the object through the periphery vision for three consecutive time steps. The task of the agent is to correctly label the category of the current letter or object during the second half of the trial, that is, when the agent has explored the image for enough time. The agent is evaluated by the fitness function FF, which is comprised of two components: the first one, $F_1(t, c)$ rewards the agent's ability to rank the correct category higher than the other categories; the second one $F_2(t, c)$ rewards the ability to maximize the activation of the correct unit while minimizing the activations of the wrong units, with the activation of the maximization of the correct unit weighting as much as the sum of the minimization of incorrect units:

$$F_1(t, c) = 2^{-rank(t,c)} \tag{5}$$

$$F_2(t,c) = 0.5 * y_r^{t,c} + \sum_{y \in y_w^t} (1-y) * \frac{0.5}{nOL-1} \tag{6}$$

$$FF = \frac{\sum_{t=1}^{nT} \sum_{c=sFC}^{nC} (0.5 * F_1(t,c) + 0.5 * F_2(t,c))}{nT * (nC - sFC)} \tag{7}$$

where $F_1(t,c)$ and $F_2(t,c)$ are the values of the two fitness components at step c of trial t, $rank(t,c)$ is the ranking of the activation of the categorization corresponding to the correct letter or object (that is, from 0, meaning the most activated and 4, meaning the least activated), $y_r^{t,c}$ is the activation of the output corresponding to the right letter or object at step c of trial t, y_w^t is the set of activations of the wrong letters or objects at step c of trial t, nOL is the number of letters or objects, nT is the number of trials, nC is the number of steps in a trial (that is, 100) and sFC is the time step in which we start to compute fitness (that is, 50). The initial population consists of 100 randomly generated genotypes, each encoding the free parameters of the corresponding neural controller, which include all the connection weights, gain factors, biases, and the time constants of leaky hidden neurons. The parameters are encoded with 8 bits each. In order to generate the phenotypes, weights and biases are linearly mapped in the range [-5,5], while time constants are mapped in [0,1].

3.1   Experiment One

The Experiment was done in order to show the effectiveness of the gray-scale method in solving a simple image classification problem (i.e. letter categorization). The experiment consists of a moving eye located in front of a screen of 100 by 100 pixels and is used to display the letters to be categorized (one at a time). The artificial eye is a periphery only, which consists of a 5 by 5 photo-receptors uniformly distributed over a square area that covers the entire retina of the eye. Each photo-receptor detects the average gray level of an area corresponding to 10 by 10 pixels of the image displayed in front of the screen. The activation of each photo-receptor ranges from 0 to 1, with 0 representing a fully white and 1 representing a fully black visual field. The screen is used to display five italic letters (l, u, n, o, j) of five different sizes each, with a variation of ± 10 and ± 20 percent to the intermediate size (see Fig. 1, for the letter l). The letters are displayed in black and gray over a white background as shown in Fig. 1.

The agent is evaluated for 50 trials, lasting 100 time steps each. At the beginning of each trial: (i) one of the five letters in one of the 5 different sizes is displayed at the center of the image screen, with each size of each letter presented twice to an individual; (ii) the state of the internal neurons are initialized to 0.0; and (iii) the eye is randomly initialized at the centre one third of the screen, so that the agent can always perceive part of the letter with the periphery vision.

3.2   Experiments Two and Three

In experiment two, we have used the Uniform Local Binary Pattern method [8] for the pre-processing of the periphery region for the task of categorizing objects in images taken from a Humanoid robot's camera; and in experiment three, we adopted the gray-scale method for the same problem. The two systems are used to categorize coloured images (320 by 240 pixels each) of five different objects namely: soft toy, tv remote control set, microphone, board wiper, and hammer. Each image of an object has five different sizes with a variation of ±10 and ±20 percent to the intermediate size; and each size is varied in five orientations in the range [+4,-4]. The total training set is of 125 images, and the original coloured images are first converted into gray images. The agents are evaluated for 250 trials lasting 100 time steps each. At the beginning of each trial: (i) each object in each image is presented twice to each individual, (ii) the state of the internal neurons are initialized to 0.0, and (iii) the eye is initialized in a random position within the central one third of the object. Also, in order to make the images suited for the systems, in which trials are terminated when the eye (periphery region) loses visual contact with the object for three consecutive time steps; we used a Canny Edge Detector to detect the edges in each image loaded per trial, and set a rectangular mask on the objects in the images, and set every white (edge) pixel outside the boundaries of these to black. Through this we are able to get edge images that consist of total outside boundaries of black, and objects of white and black. Figure 2 shows the gray images, Fig. 3 shows the images after being processed by the Canny Edge Detector and Fig. 4 shows the images after setting rectangular masks on the Canny Edge Detector processed images. It should be noted that the above processing of the gray images by Canny Edge Detector and rectangular masking, which finally led to the images shown in Fig. 4 are only used to control the movement of the eye, so that every trial is terminated after the periphery vision loses total focus of the object for more than 3 consecutive time steps. It is the gray images that are processed by the Uniform Local Binary Pattern [8] (Experiment Two), and gray-scale averaging (Experiment Three), and are used as input vector to the Neural Network along with efferent copies of the movement and categorization units (that is, activations at previous time step $t - 1$).

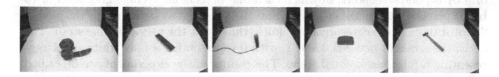

Fig. 2. The above figure shows the gray images that are used in the categorization experiments (Color figure online)

Fig. 3. The above figure shows the images after being processed by the Canny Edge Detector

Fig. 4. The above figure shows the images after setting rectangular masks on the Canny Edge Detector processed gray images (Color figure online)

Experiment Two. The experimental set up consists of a moving eye (artificial agent), covering a total area of 50 by 50 pixels (periphery region) of the presented image per trial. The periphery image region is pre-processed with Uniform Local Binary Pattern [8], in order to enhance its quality and also to reduce the feature vector size. In the experiment, we have divided the periphery region into 4 blocks, in which histograms of uniform patterns are constructed for each block. Histograms of all the blocks are concatenated to form a feature vector, with each block giving a histogram of size 59. The feature vector is normalized to sum to 1, to give a probability distribution of Uniform Local Binary Patterns, with 1 representing maximum distribution of patterns and 0 for no pattern; which forms the input vector of the neural network along with the efferent copies of the movement and categorization output units

Experiment Three. We performed a third experiment in-order to do a comparative analysis of the results with the results from our proposed method in Experiment Two. In this experiment, we adopted the gray-scale averaging method in [1] for the processing of the periphery region of the images taken from the Humanoid robot camera. The Neural Network has the following inputs: (i) the activations of 5 by 5 photo-receptors, in which each one detects an average gray level of 10 by 10 pixels of the image displayed; and (ii) the efferent copies of the outputs of 2 motor units and 5 categorization units (that is, at the previous time step). The activations ranges between 0 and 1, with 0 representing a fully white and 1 representing a fully black visual scene. The results of the experiment are described in Sect. 4.

4   Results

We show here the results of our experiments separately, as we have performed three major experiments.

4.1 Experiment One

We have performed 10 replications of the evolutionary run, (Fig. 5 shows the graph of the best fitness); and also assessed the categorization capability of the system for the five letters (l, u, n, o, j) in the evaluation test (Table 1). We have used 25 image datasets in the evaluation stage, with each letter of different size from the one used in the training stage, and of a variation of 3 to 15 percent of the intermediate size. The system was evaluated for about 100000 trials for proper generalization. The replicated gray-scale averaging experiment did very well in the task of categorizing all the letters as demonstrated by higher average activations of the current categories than those of the other categories. The average performance accuracy in all categorization tasks was about 95 percent.

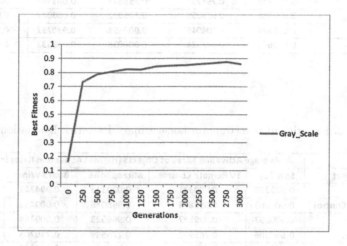

Fig. 5. The average of the best fitness in 10 replications of the evolutionary run for the Experiment *One*

4.2 Experiment Two

We have also shown here the results of the performance evaluation test of our proposed Uniform Local Binary Patten method [8], for 10 replications of the evolutionary run (Fig. 6). The evaluation test was done for a set of 5 objects, namely: soft toy, tv remote control, microphone, board wiper and hammer; on images taken from a humanoid robot camera. Each object is of 2 different sizes, with a variation of 10 and 20 percent to the intermediate size, and each size of 5 different orientations in the range [+3,-3]. The total evaluation sets are 50 images. The assessment of the performance of the system was done using average of activations of each labelled category for about 100000 trials (Table 2). The results from our evaluation test show that the system was able to categorize the tv remote control and board wiper, and did fairly well for others; especially that of the soft-toy, of which its average activation value was slightly lower than that of the highest one. In the case of incorrect categorization of the current categories (soft toy, microphone and hammer), the differences between average activations of the current categories and the higher average activations were very small. Overall the system has an average performance accuracy of about 50 percent in all categorization tasks (Fig. 7).

Table 1. Experiment one (Gray-scale): Evaluation test

Current Letters	Average Activation Rates of Letters (Highest Activation Rates in Bold)				
	l	u	n	o	j
l	**0.950000**	0.748170	0.000017	0.006498	0.031623
u	0.009783	**0.793737**	0.259696	0.005544	0.033172
n	0.000736	0.673059	**0.875992**	0.006077	0.029533
o	0.018844	0.004046	0.000151	**0.930732**	0.161261
j	0.096664	0.002624	0.000038	0.008332	**0.885962**

Table 2. Experiment two (Uniform Local Binary Pattern): Evaluation test

Current Object	Average Activation Rates of Objects (Highest Activation Rates in Bold)				
	Soft Toy	TV Remote Control	Microphone	Board Wiper	Hammer
Soft Toy	0.975220	0.000331	0.000313	**0.994261**	0.000011
TV Remote Control	0.000065	**0.999845**	0.968086	0.000453	0.905323
Microphone	0.000057	**0.999847**	0.966523	0.000464	0.901004
Board Wiper	0.696386	0.285902	0.276539	**0.710205**	0.256889
Hammer	0.000061	**0.999845**	0.967011	0.000444	0.907568

Table 3. Experiment three (Gray-Scale): Evaluation test

Current Objects	Average Activation Rates of Objects (Highest Activation Rates in Bold)				
	Soft Toy	TV Remote Control	Microphone	Board Wiper	Hammer
Soft Toy	**1.000000**	0.999250	0.000139	0.994623	0.999973
TV Remote Control	**1.000000**	0.999250	0.000138	0.994623	0.999973
Microphone	**1.000000**	0.999250	0.000138	0.994623	0.999973
Board Wiper	**1.000000**	0.999250	0.000138	0.994623	0.999973
Hammer	**1.000000**	0.999250	0.000138	0.994623	0.999973

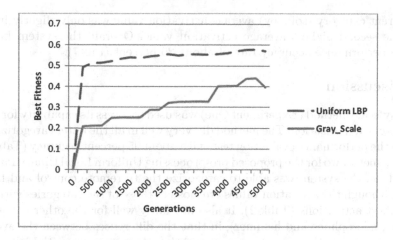

Fig. 6. Shows the average of the best fitness of 10 replications of the evolutionary run for the Uniform Local Binary Patterns [8] Experiment Two, and gray-scale Experiment Three for categorization of the objects on the images taken from Humanoid (iCub) robot camera (Color figure online).

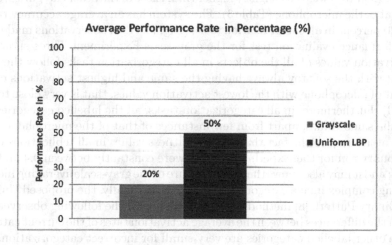

Fig. 7. The chart shows the average performance accuracy for the gray-scale and Uniform Local Binary Pattern method [8] in categorizing objects taken from the Humanoid iCub robots camera in 100000 trials (Color figure online).

4.3 Experiment Three

We have performed 10 replications of the evolutionary run (Fig. 6). The performance of the system was evaluated based on average of activations of each labelled category in about 100000 trials (Table 3). We used the same set of data of the evaluation stage in Experiment Two, in order to make adequate and unbiased comparison. The results show that the gray-scale method was able to categorize only the soft toy; and even in the case of correct categorization, the current category (soft toy) average activation value was only slightly higher than the second highest average activation value. Overall, the system has an average performance accuracy rate of about 20 percent (Fig. 7).

5 Discussion

The gray-scale method (Experiment One) was used to assess its capability for ordinary letter categorization. The method did very well in all the letter categorization tasks in the performance evaluation test, with about 95 percent accuracy (Table 1). In Experiment Two for the proposed pre-processing Uniform Local Binary Pattern Method [8], the system was able to categorize the tv remote control and board wiper; although the activation values are close to those of the categories with second highest activations (Table 2). It also did fairly well for the other categories (soft toy, microphone and hammer), in that the differences between the average activation values of the current category and the other categories with higher activations are quite small. Overall the system has an average accuracy rate of about 50 percent (Fig. 7). The gray-scale method in Experiment three was only able to categorize the soft toy; and in this case, the average activation value of the current category (soft toy) was only slightly higher than those of the other categories, apart from that of the microphone (Table 3). The system has an average accuracy rate of about 20 percent in all categorization tasks (Fig. 7). Also, observations made from the performance evaluation test for the gray-scale Experiment Three show that the activation values of all the objects in all categorization tasks follow the same pattern; with the soft toy always having the same and highest activations of 1.0, and that of microphone with the lowest activation values, that is very close to zero (Table 3). Furthermore, in all categorization tasks, all the labelled categories had about the same values, apart from few instances of that of the microphone. This may be attributed to the fact that the best fitness values in all replications of the evolutionary run for the Experiment Three were constantly between 0.4 and 0.45 (Fig. 6); and it may also shows the erratic nature of the gray-scale averaging method in solving complex image categorization problems. Finally, the proposed Uniform Local Binary Pattern [8] method is very promising for the following observed reasons: (i) the differences between the average activation rates of the current category and the other labelled categories are very small for incorrect categorizations; (ii) the current category always gives high activations, even for the incorrect classifications. We therefore, have an intuition that if the eye could be better controlled to detect the most salient region per time for subsequent processing, we may be able to improve further and achieve better results than the gray-scale method, and so adapt the system to work in a variety of categorization tasks. Future work will be in this direction.

6 Conclusion

We have investigated using Uniform Local Binary Patterns [8] for pre-processing more complex images taken from Humanoid iCub robot camera for a Neuro-Evolution controlled Active Vision System. Our proposed method had about

50 percent accuracy as compared to gray-scale method of about 20 percent in the same categorization tasks. Future research will be done in bottom up models for filtering features such as colour, intensity and orientation of pixels in generating saliency maps, in order to detect salient region in a visual scene; thereby giving a more intelligent control of the eye for subsequent processing.

References

1. Mirolli, M., Ferrauto, T., Nolfi, S.: Categorisation through evidence accumulation in an active vision system. Connect. Sci. **22**, 331–354 (2010)
2. Aditya, K., Nakul, I.: Evolving An Active Vision System for Constrained Environments. AI Project Report (2010)
3. Floreano, D., Kato, T., Marocco, D., Sauser, E.: Co-evolution of active vision and feature selection. Biol. Cybernet. **90**, 218–228 (2004)
4. Stanley, K.O., Miikkulainen, R.: Evolving a roving eye for go. In: Deb, K., Tari, Z. (eds.) GECCO 2004. LNCS, vol. 3103, pp. 1226–1238. Springer, Heidelberg (2004)
5. James, D., Tucker, P.: Evolving a neural network active vision system for shape discrimination. In: Genetic and Evolutionary Computation Conference (2005)
6. Morimoto, G., Ikegami, T.: Evolution of plastic sensory-motor coupling and dynamic categorization. Artif. Life **9**, 188–193 (2005)
7. Tuci, E.: Evolutionary swarm robotics: genetic diversity, task-allocation and task-switching. In: Dorigo, M., Birattari, M., Garnier, S., Hamann, H., Montes de Oca, M., Solnon, C., Stützle, T. (eds.) ANTS 2014. LNCS, vol. 8667, pp. 98–109. Springer, Heidelberg (2014)
8. Ojala, T., Pietikinen, M., Maenpaa, T.: Multi-resolution gray-scale and rotation invariant texture classification with local binary patterns. IEEE Transact. Patt. Anal. Mach. Intell. **29**, 51–59 (2002)

Learning in Networked Interactions:
A Replicator Dynamics Approach

Daan Bloembergen[1,2]([✉]), Ipek Caliskanelli[1], and Karl Tuyls[1]

[1] Department of Computer Science, University of Liverpool, Liverpool, UK
{d.bloembergen,ipek.caliskanelli,k.tuyls}@liverpool.ac.uk
[2] Department of Knowledge Engineering, Maastricht University,
Maastricht, The Netherlands

Abstract. Many real-world scenarios can be modelled as multi-agent systems, where multiple autonomous decision makers interact in a single environment. The complex and dynamic nature of such interactions prevents hand-crafting solutions for all possible scenarios, hence learning is crucial. Studying the dynamics of multi-agent learning is imperative in selecting and tuning the right learning algorithm for the task at hand. So far, analysis of these dynamics has been mainly limited to normal form games, or unstructured populations. However, many multi-agent systems are highly structured, complex networks, with agents only interacting locally. Here, we study the dynamics of such networked interactions, using the well-known replicator dynamics of evolutionary game theory as a model for learning. Different learning algorithms are modelled by altering the replicator equations slightly. In particular, we investigate lenience as an enabler for cooperation. Moreover, we show how well-connected, stubborn agents can influence the learning outcome. Finally, we investigate the impact of structural network properties on the learning outcome, as well as the influence of mutation driven by exploration.

Keywords: Reinforcement learning · Social networks · Replicator dynamics

1 Introduction

Understanding the dynamics of networked interactions is of vital importance to a wide range of research areas. For example, these dynamics play a central role in biological systems such as the human brain [10] or molecular interaction networks within cells [4]; in large technological systems such as the word wide web [16]; in social networks such as Facebook [2,18,37]; and in economic or financial institutions such as the stock market [12,22]. Recently, researchers have focused on studying the evolution of cooperation in networks of self-interested individuals, aiming to understand how cooperative behaviour can be sustained in the face of individual selfishness [21,26,30,31].

Many studies have targeted the discovery of structural properties of networks that promote cooperation. For instance, Santos and Pecheco show that cooperation has a higher chance of survival in scale-free networks [31]; Ohtsuki et al.

© Springer International Publishing Switzerland 2015
C.J. Headleand et al. (Eds.): ALIA 2014, CCIS 519, pp. 44–58, 2015.
DOI: 10.1007/978-3-319-18084-7_4

find a relation between the cost-benefit ratio of cooperation and the average node degree of a network that determines whether cooperation can be sustained [27]; and Van Segbroeck et al. investigate heterogeneity and clustering and concludes that these structural properties influence behaviour on the individual rather than the overall network [38]. Others have focused on the role of the particular interaction model between neighbouring nodes in determining the success of cooperation. For example, Hofmann et al. simulate various update rules in different network topologies and find that the evolution of cooperation is highly dependent on the combination of update mechanism and network topology [21].

Cooperation can also be promoted using some incentivising structure in which defection is punishable [9,32], or in which players can choose beforehand to commit to cooperation for some given cost [19]. Both incentives increase the willingness to cooperate in such scenarios where defection would be individually rational otherwise. Allowing individuals to choose with whom to interact may similarly sustain cooperation, e.g. by giving individuals the possibility to break ties with 'bad' neighbours and replacing them with a random new connection. For example, Zimmermann and Eguíluz show how such a mechanism may promote cooperation, albeit sensitive to perturbations [42]. Similarly, Edmonds et al. use a tag-based system through which agents identify whom to interact with [17]. Allowing agents to choose which tag to adopt gives rise to social structures that can enhance cooperation. Finally, control theory is used by Bloembergen et al. to show how external influence on a subset of nodes can drive the behaviour in social networks [7].

Most of these works share one important limitation, in that they consider only imitation-based learning dynamics. Typically in such models, individual agents update their behaviour by replicating the successful behaviour of their peers. In evolution terms, the update process only incorporates *selection*. However, evolutionary success often stems from the interplay between selection on the one hand, and *mutation* on the other. Closely related is the *exploration/exploitation* dilemma that is well-known in the field of reinforcement learning, where exploration plays the role of mutation, and exploitation yield selection.

Here, we bridge these two interpretations by analysing selection-mutation dynamics as a predictive model for multi-agent reinforcement learning, where interaction between agents is modelled as a structured social network. In particular, we investigate *lenience* [6,29] as an enabler for cooperation. We report a great difference between pure selection dynamics, and selection-mutation dynamics that include leniency. Moreover, we show how a subset of *stubborn* agents can influence the learning outcome. We find that well connected agents exert a large influence on the overall network behaviour, and as such can drive the learning process towards a desired outcome. Furthermore, we show how structural network properties, such as size and average degree, influence the learning outcome. Finally, we observe that certain network structures give rise to clusters of cooperators and defectors coexisting.

In contrast to the majority of related work, which almost exclusively focuses on Prisoner's Dilemma type interactions, we use the Stag Hunt to describe the interaction between agents. The Stag Hunt provides an intuitive model of many real-world strategic (economic) interactions, such as the introduction of potentially beneficial new technologies that require a critical mass of adopters in order to pay off. As such, not switching (defecting) is a safe choice, whereas social cooperation (adoption) may yield higher rewards for all.

This paper proceeds as follows. Firstly, we explain required background knowledge on learning, evolutionary game theory, and networks, in Sect. 2. Secondly, Sect. 3 outlines the methodology used in this work, in particular the formal link between multi-agent learning and the replicator dynamics. We present our model of networked replicator dynamics in Sect. 4, accompanied by a range of experiments in Sect. 5. The paper is closed with main conclusion of this study in Sect. 6.

2   Background

This section gives an overview of relevant background needed for the remainder of this work. The section is split into three main parts. Section 2.1 briefly introduces reinforcement learning; Sect. 2.2 describes basic concepts of evolutionary game theory; and Sect. 2.3 details networks.

2.1   Reinforcement Learning

The *reinforcement learning* (RL) paradigm is based on the concept of trial-and-error learning, allowing agents to optimise their behaviour without explicitly requiring a model of the environment [34]. The reinforcement learning agent continuously interacts with the environment, perceiving its state, taking actions, and observing the effect of those actions. The agent needs to balance *exploration* and *exploitation* in order to ensure good intermediate rewards while avoiding getting stuck in local optima. RL strategies are powerful techniques for optimising control of large scale control problems [15]. Early RL research focused on single-agent problems where the full state knowledge of the agent is known. Later on, RL has been applied to multi-agent domains as well [11]. The computational complexity of *multi-agent reinforcement learning* (MARL) algorithms is much higher than in single-agent problems, since (near) optimal behaviour of one agent depends on other agents' policies as well.

Despite this challenge, single-agent RL techniques have been applied successfully to multi-agent settings. Arguably the most famous example of an RL algorithm is the model-free temporal difference algorithm *Q-learning* [39]. Q-learning[1] maintains a value function over actions, Q_i, which is updated at every time step t based on the reward r received after taking action a_i:

$$Q_i(t+1) \leftarrow Q_i(t) + \alpha\big(r - Q_i(t)\big) \tag{1}$$

---

[1] We describe *stateless* Q-learning, as this version is suitable for the work presented in this paper.

where $\alpha \in [0, 1]$ is the learning rate that determines how quickly Q is updated based on new reward information. Choosing which action to take is crucial for the learning process. The *Boltzmann* exploration scheme is often used as it provides a way to balance exploration and exploitation by selecting an appropriate temperature τ. The policy $\mathbf{x}$ that determines the probability for choosing each action a is computed as

$$x_i = \frac{e^{Q_i/\tau}}{\sum_j e^{Q_j/\tau}} \tag{2}$$

A high temperature drives the mechanism towards exploration, whereas a low temperature promotes exploitation.

2.2 Evolutionary Game Theory

The strategic interaction between agents can be modelled in the form of a game, where each player (agent) has a set of actions, and a preference over the joint action space that is captured in the received payoffs. For two-player games, the payoffs can be represented by a bi-matrix $(\mathbf{A}, \mathbf{B})$, that gives the payoff for the row player in $\mathbf{A}$, and the column player in $\mathbf{B}$, see Fig. 1 (left). The goal of each player is to decide which action to take, so as to maximise their expected payoff. Classical game theory assumes that full knowledge of the game is available to all players, which together with the assumption of individual rationality does not necessarily reflect the dynamic nature of real world interaction. *Evolutionary game theory* (EGT) relaxes the rationality assumption and replaces it by the concepts of natural selection and mutation from evolutionary biology [24, 41]. Where classical game theory describes strategies in the form of probabilities over pure actions, EGT models them as populations of individuals, each of a pure action type, where the population share of each type reflects its evolutionary success.

$$\begin{pmatrix} a_{11}, b_{11} & a_{12}, b_{12} \\ a_{21}, b_{21} & a_{22}, b_{22} \end{pmatrix} \quad \begin{matrix} & C & D \\ C & \\ D & \end{matrix}\begin{pmatrix} A, A & C, B \\ B, C & D, D \end{pmatrix} \quad \begin{matrix} & C & D \\ C & \\ D & \end{matrix}\begin{pmatrix} 4, 4 & 1, 3 \\ 3, 1 & 3, 3 \end{pmatrix}$$

Fig. 1. General payoff bi-matrix $(\mathbf{A}, \mathbf{B})$ for two-player two-action games (left) and the Stag Hunt (center), and a typically valued instance of the Stag Hunt (right)

Central to EGT are the *replicator dynamics*, that describe how this population of individuals evolves over time under evolutionary pressure. Individuals are randomly paired to interact, and their reproductive success is determined by their fitness which results from these interactions. The replicator dynamics dictate that the population share of a certain type will increase if the individuals of this type have a higher fitness than the population average; otherwise their population share will decrease. The population can be described by the state vector $\mathbf{x} = (x_1, x_2, \ldots, x_n)^{\mathrm{T}}$, with $0 \leq x_i \leq 1$ $\forall i$ and $\sum_i x_i = 1$, representing the fractions of the population belonging to each of n pure types. Now suppose the fitness of type i is given by the fitness function $f_i(\mathbf{x})$, and the average fitness of the population is given by $\bar{f}(\mathbf{x}) = \sum_j x_j f_j(\mathbf{x})$. The population change over time can then be written as

$$\dot{x}_i = x_i \left[f_i(\mathbf{x}) - \bar{f}(\mathbf{x}) \right] \tag{3}$$

In a two-player game with payoff bi-matrix $(\mathbf{A}, \mathbf{B})$, where the two players use the strategies $\mathbf{x}$ and $\mathbf{y}$ respectively, the fitness of the first player's i^{th} candidate strategy can be calculated as $\sum_j a_{ij} y_j$. Similarly, the average fitness of population $\mathbf{x}$ is defined as $\sum_i x_i \sum_j a_{ij} y_j$. In matrix form, this leads to the following multi-population replicator dynamics:

$$\begin{aligned} \dot{x}_i &= x_i \left[(\mathbf{A}\mathbf{y})_i - \mathbf{x}^{\mathrm{T}} \mathbf{A} \mathbf{y} \right] \\ \dot{y}_i &= y_i \left[(\mathbf{x}^{\mathrm{T}} \mathbf{B})_i - \mathbf{x}^{\mathrm{T}} \mathbf{B} \mathbf{y} \right] \end{aligned} \tag{4}$$

The Stag Hunt is a game that describes a dilemma between safety and social cooperation [33]. The canonical payoff matrix of the Stag Hunt is given in Fig. 1 (center), where $A > B \geq D > C$. Social cooperation between players is rewarded with A, given that both players choose to cooperate (action C). As the players do not foresee each others' strategies, the safe choice of players is to defect (action D), since typically $A + C < B + D$ (see Fig. 1, right). Although cooperation pays off more for both players, defection is individually rational when the opponent strategy is unknown. As both players reason like this, they may end up in a state of mutual defection, receiving $D < A$ each, hence the dilemma.

The Stag Hunt is typically said to model individuals that go out on a hunt, and can only capture big game (e.g. a stag) by joining forces, whereas smaller pray (e.g. a hare) can be captured individually. However, it can also be thought of to describe the introduction of a new technology, which only really pays off when more people are using it. Early adopters risk paying the price for this. As such, despite its simplicity the Stag Hunt is an useful model for many real-world strategic dilemmas.

2.3   Networked Interactions

Networks describe collections of entities (nodes) and the relation between them (edges). Formally, a network can be represented by a graph $\mathbb{G} = (\mathcal{V}, \mathcal{W})$ consisting of a non-empty set of nodes (or vertices) $\mathcal{V} = \{v_1, \ldots, v_N\}$ and an $N \times N$ adjacency matrix $\mathcal{W} = [w_{ij}]$ where non-zero entries w_{ij} indicate the (possibly weighted) connection from v_i to v_j. If $\mathcal{W}$ is symmetrical, such that $w_{ij} = w_{ji}$ for all i, j, the graph is said to be undirected, meaning that the connection from node v_i to v_j is equal to the connection from node v_j to v_i. In social networks, for example, one might argue that friendship is usually mutual and hence undirected. This is the approach followed in this work. In general however this need not be the case, in which case the graph is said to be directed, and $\mathcal{W}$ asymmetrical. The neighbourhood, $\mathbb{N}$, of a node v_i is defined as the set of nodes it is directly connected to, i.e. $\mathbb{N}(v_i) = \cup_j v_j : w_{ij} > 0$. The node's degree $\deg[v_i]$ is given by the cardinality of its neighbourhood.

Several types of networks have been proposed that capture the structural properties found in large social, technological or biological networks, two well-known examples being the small-world and scale-free models. The *small-world* model exhibits short average path lengths between nodes and high clustering, two features often found in real-world networks [40]. Another model is the *scale-free* network, characterised by a heavy-tailed degree distribution following a power law [3]. In such networks the majority of nodes will have a small degree while simultaneously there will be relatively many nodes with very large degree, the latter being the hubs or connectors of the network. For a detailed description of networks and their properties, the interested reader is referred to [22].

3   Evolutionary Models of Multi-agent Learning

Multi-agent learning and evolutionary game theory share a substantial part of their foundation, in that they both deal with the decision making process of bounded rational agents, or players, in uncertain environments. The link between these two fields is not only intuitive, but also formally proven that the continuous time limit of *Cross learning* converges to the replicator dynamics [8].

Cross learning [14] is one of the most basic stateless reinforcement learning algorithms, which updates its policy $\mathbf{x}$ based on the reward r received after taking action j as

$$x_i \leftarrow x_i + \begin{cases} r - x_i r \text{ if } i = j \\ -x_i r \quad \text{otherwise} \end{cases} \tag{5}$$

A valid policy is ensured by the update rule as long as the rewards are normalised, i.e., $0 \leq r \leq 1$. Cross learning is closely related to learning automata (LA) [25,35]. In particular, it is equivalent to a learning automaton with a linear reward-inaction (L_{R-I}) update scheme and a learning step size of 1.

We can estimate $E[\Delta x_i]$, the expected change in the policy induced by Eq. 5. Note that the probability x_i of action i is affected both if i is selected and if another action j is selected, and let $E_i[r]$ be the expected reward after taking action i. We can now write

$$E[\Delta x_i] = x_i \Big[E_i[r] - x_i E_i[r] \Big] + \sum_{j \neq i} x_j \Big[- E_j[r]x_i \Big]$$
$$= x_i \Big[E_i[r] - \sum_j x_j E_j[r] \Big] \tag{6}$$

Assuming the learner takes infinitesimally small update steps, we can take the continuous time limit of Eq. 6 and write is as the partial differential equation

$$\dot{x}_i = x_i \Big[E_i[r] - \sum_j x_j E_j[r] \Big]$$

In a two-player normal form game, with payoff matrix $\mathbf{A}$ and policies $\mathbf{x}$ and $\mathbf{y}$ for the two players, respectively, this yields

$$\dot{x}_i = x_i \Big[(\mathbf{Ay})_i - \mathbf{x}^\mathrm{T} \mathbf{Ay} \Big] \tag{7}$$

which are exactly the multi-population replicator dynamics of Eq. 4.

The dynamical model of Eq. 7 only describes the evolutionary process of *selection*, as Cross learning does not incorporate an exploration mechanism. However, in many scenarios *mutation* also plays a role, where individuals not only reproduce, but may change their behaviour while doing so. Given a population $\mathbf{x}$ as defined above, we consider a mutation rate $\mathcal{E}_{ij}$ indicating the propensity of species j to mutate into i (note the order of the indices), such that, $\forall i$:

$$\mathcal{E}_{ij} \geq 0 \quad \text{and} \quad \sum_i \mathcal{E}_{ij} = 1$$

Adding mutation to Eq. 7 leads to a dynamical model with separate selection and mutation terms [20], given by

$$\dot{x}_i = x_i \underbrace{\left[(\mathbf{Ay})_i - \mathbf{x}^T\mathbf{Ay}\right]}_{\text{selection}} + \underbrace{\sum_j \left(\mathcal{E}_{ij}x_j - \mathcal{E}_{ji}x_i\right)}_{\text{mutation}} \tag{8}$$

By slightly altering or extending the model of Eq. 7 different RL algorithms can be modelled as well. A selection-mutation model of Boltzmann Q-learning (Eqs. 1 and 2) has been proposed by Tuyls et al. [36]. The dynamical system can again be decomposed into terms for exploitation (selection following the replicator dynamics) and exploration (mutation through randomization based on the Boltzmann mechanism):

$$\dot{x}_i = \frac{\alpha x_i}{\tau} \underbrace{\left[(\mathbf{Ay})_i - \mathbf{x}^T\mathbf{Ay}\right]}_{\text{selection}} - \alpha x_i \underbrace{\left[\log x_i - \sum_k x_k \log x_k\right]}_{\text{mutation}} \tag{9}$$

Technically, these dynamics model the variant Frequency Adjusted Q-learning (FAQ), which mimics simultaneous action updates [23].

Lenient FAQ-learning (LFAQ) [6] is a variation aimed at overcoming convergence to suboptimal equilibria by mis-coordination in the early phase of the learning process, when mistakes by one agent may lead to penalties for others, irrespective of the quality of their actions. Leniency towards such mistakes can be achieved by collecting κ rewards for each action, and updating the Q-value based on the highest of those rewards. This causes an (optimistic) change in the expected reward for the actions of the learning agent, incorporating the probability of a potential reward for that action being the highest of κ consecutive tries [29]. The expected reward for each action $\mathbf{Ay}$ in Eq. 9 is replaced by the utility vector $\mathbf{u}$, with

$$u_i = \sum_j \frac{a_{ij}y_j\left[\left(\sum_{k:a_{ik}\leq a_{ij}} y_k\right)^\kappa - \left(\sum_{k:a_{ik}<a_{ij}} y_k\right)^\kappa\right]}{\sum_{k:a_{ik}=a_{ij}} y_k} \tag{10}$$

Each of these models approximates the learning process of independent reinforcement learners in a multi-agent setting. Specifically, they are presented for the case of two-agent interacting in a normal-form game. Extensions to n-players are straightforward, but fall outside the scope of this work. In the next section we will describe our extension of networked replicator dynamics.

Algorithm 1. Update procedure for the NRD model

1: initialize $\mathcal{X}$
2: $\dot{\mathcal{X}} \leftarrow \mathbf{0}$
3: **for** $j = 1$ to N **do**
4:     **for all** $\mathbf{x}^k \in \mathbb{N}(v_j)$ **do**
5:        $\dot{x}_i^j \leftarrow \dot{x}_i^j + x_i^j \left[(\mathbf{A}\mathbf{x}^k)_i - \mathbf{x}^{j\mathrm{T}} \mathbf{A}\mathbf{x}^k \right]$
6:     **end for**
7:     $\dot{\mathbf{x}}^j \leftarrow \frac{\dot{\mathbf{x}}^j}{|\mathbb{N}(v_j)|}$
8: **end for**
9: $\mathcal{X} \leftarrow \mathcal{X} + \dot{\mathcal{X}}$
---

4 Networked Replicator Dynamics

In this work, agents are placed on the nodes of a network, and interact only locally with their direct neighbours. Assume a graph $\mathbb{G}$ with N nodes as defined in Sect. 2.3, with N agents placed on the nodes $\{v_1, \ldots, v_N\}$. If we define each agent by its current policy $\mathbf{x}$ we can write the current network state $\mathcal{X} = (\mathbf{x}^1, \ldots, \mathbf{x}^N)$. The aim of this work is study how $\mathcal{X}$ evolves over time, given the specific network structure and learning model of the agents. For this purpose, we introduce *networked replicator dynamics* (NRD), where each agent (or node) is modelled by a population of pure strategies, interacting with each if its neighbours following the multi-population replicator dynamics of Eq. 4.

The update mechanism of the proposed networked replicator dynamics is given in Algorithm 1. At every time step, each agent (line 3) interacts with each of its neighbours (line 4) by playing a symmetric normal-form game defined by payoff-matrix $\mathbf{A}$. These interactions are modelled by the replicator dynamics (line 5), where each neighbour incurs a potential population change, $\dot{\mathbf{x}}$, in the agent. Those changes are normalised by the degree, $|\mathbb{N}(v_i)|$, of the agent's node (line 7). Finally, all agents update their state (line 9).

This model is flexible in that it is independent of the network structure, it can be used to simulate any symmetric normal form game, and different replicator models can easily be plugged in (line 5 of Algorithm 1). This means that we can use any of the dynamical models presented in Sect. 3 as update rule, thereby simulating different MARL algorithms.

5 Experimental Validation

In this section we present experimental results of the networked replicator dynamics model in various setups. In particular, we use Barabási-Albert *scale-free* [3] and Watts-Strogatz *small world* [40] networks. The first set of experiments compares the different learning models, focusing in particular on the role of exploration and lenience in the learning process. We then analyse lenience in more detail, investigating the influence of the degree of lenience on the speed of convergence. Hereafter, we look at the relation between network size and degree with respect to the equilibrium outcome. The last set of experiments investigates the role of stubborn nodes, which do not update their strategy, on the resulting network dynamics. All experiments use the Stag Hunt (page 4, Fig. 1, right) as the model of interaction.

5.1 Comparing Different Learning Models

We compare the different dynamical models of multi-agent learning presented before in Sect. 3. We use the following abbreviations: CL is Cross learning (Eq. 7); CL+ is CL with mutation (Eq. 8); FAQ is frequency adjusted Q-learning (Eq. 9); LF-κ is lenient FAQ with degree of lenience κ (Eq. 10). In order to ensure smooth dynamics we multiply the update $\dot{\mathbf{x}}$ of each model by a step size α. CL and CL+ use $\alpha = 0.5$, FAQ uses $\alpha = 0.1$, and LF uses $\alpha = 0.2$. Moreover, the exploration (mutation) rates are set as follows: CL+ uses $\mathcal{E}_{ij} = 0.01$ for all $i \neq j$, and $\mathcal{E}_{ii} = 1 - \sum_{j \neq i} \mathcal{E}_{ij}$; and FAQ and LF use $\tau = 0.1$. We simulate the model on 100 randomly generated networks of $N = 50$ nodes (both scale free and small world, the latter with rewiring probability $p = 0.5$), starting from 50 random initial states $\mathcal{X} \in \mathbb{R}^N$, and report the average network state $\bar{\mathcal{X}} = \frac{1}{N}\sum_i \mathbf{x}^i$ after convergence. Since the Stag Hunt only has two actions, the full state can be defined by x_1, the probability of the first action (cooperate).

Figure 2 shows the results of this comparison. The gray scale indicates the final network state $\bar{\mathcal{X}}$ after convergence, where black means defection, and white means cooperation. Note the non-linear scale, this is chosen to highlight the details in the low and high ranges of $\bar{\mathcal{X}}$. Several observations can be made based on these results. First of all, there is a clear distinction between non-lenient algorithms, which converge mostly to defection, and lenient algorithms that converge toward cooperation. As expected, lenience indeed promotes cooperation also in a networked interactions. Equally striking is the lack of distinction between pure selection (CL) and selection-mutation (CL+, FAQ) models. Adding mutation (or exploration) in this setting has no effect on the resulting convergence. Increasing the mutation rate does lead to a change at some point, however, this is to the exten that the added randomness automatically drives the equilibrium away from a state of pure defection.

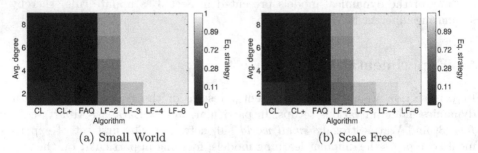

(a) Small World   (b) Scale Free

Fig. 2. Dynamics of a networked Stag Hunt game in small world and scale free networks. The figure shows the mean network state in equilibrium (gray scale) for different algorithms (x-axis) and average network degree (y-axis) (Color figure online).

The most interesting results of Fig. 2 are those of LF-2. Here, we can observe a range of outcomes, depending on the average network degree. A more strongly connected network yields a higher probability of cooperation in equilibrium. Moreover, LF-2 is the only algorithm that yield an "indecisive" final state, that is significantly removed from pure cooperation or defection. In order to investigate this situation further, we look in detail at the dynamics of a single network. Figure 3a shows the network state $\mathcal{X}$ over time for one specific (randomly drawn) initial state of a scale free network with average degree 2. Clearly, the network is split into clusters of cooperators and defectors, no unanimous outcome is reached. The final state is highlighted in Fig. 3b, depicting the network structure and state of each node, and clearly showing two clusters. Depending on initial conditions, different splits can be observed.

Similar results can be observed in small world networks. Figures 3c and d show the dynamics in an example network with average degree 4. Again, a cluster of defectors is maintained in equilibrium amongst a majority of cooperators. Identifying specific structural network properties that lead to clustering is a main question for future work.

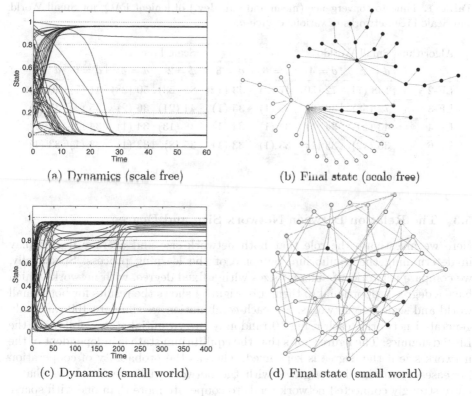

(a) Dynamics (scale free)   (b) Final state (scale free)

(c) Dynamics (small world)   (d) Final state (small world)

Fig. 3. Example of the convergence of LF-2 on a Scale Free (top) and Small World (bottom) network with average degree 2 and 4, respectively. The network is split between cooperators (white) and defectors (black) in the final equilibrium state (Color figure online).

5.2   The Effect of Lenience on Convergence

In this set of experiments, we take a closer look at the influence of leniency on the dynamics and convergence of the network. Using the same set of networks as in the previous section, we zoom in only on the lenient algorithms and compare their convergence speed for the different networks. Table 1 lists the number of time steps to convergence, again averaged over 100 networks with 50 random initial states. Two trends are clearly visible: increasing the degree of lenience decreases the convergence time (most notably for degree 2 networks); and increasing the network degree similarly decreases the convergence time (most notably for LF-2). These results can be explained intuitively, as lenience pushes the learning process in the direction of cooperation, whereas a higher network degree yield more interactions per time step, and hence faster convergence. The fact that no convergence below 33 time steps is observed, independent of the network type, can be explained by the limit that the step size α and the inherent dynamics of the model pose.

Table 1. Time to convergence (mean and std. dev.) of lenient FAQ, for Small World and Scale Free networks of various degree d.

Algorithm	Small World				Scale Free			
	$d = 2$	$d = 4$	$d = 6$	$d = 8$	$d = 2$	$d = 4$	$d = 6$	$d = 8$
LF-2	148 (71)	72 (50)	47 (21)	43 (12)	81 (53)	50 (28)	41 (7)	40 (6)
LF-3	72 (58)	36 (3)	35 (1)	35 (1)	44 (21)	36 (2)	35 (2)	35 (1)
LF-4	43 (24)	34 (1)	34 (1)	34 (1)	38 (13)	34 (1)	34 (1)	34 (1)
LF-6	35 (12)	33 (1)	33 (1)	33 (1)	35 (8)	33 (1)	33 (1)	33 (1)

5.3   The Relation Between Network Size and Degree

Here we investigate the role that both network size and average degree play in determining the equilibrium outcome of the learning process. Specifically, we compare networks of different sizes with a fixed degree, with networks which have a degree proportional to their size. Figure 4 shows the results for both small world and scale free networks. For each combination we simulate 100 randomly generated networks, each using 10 randomly drawn initial states, following the LF-2 dynamics. The figure shows that the equilibrium state is independent of the network size if the degree is kept fixed, whereas the probability of cooperation increases when the degree grows with the network. This result shows that a more strongly connected network tends to cooperate more than one with sparse interactions. Intuitively, this can be explained by the inherent dynamics of the Stag Hunt: a critical mass of cooperators is required for cooperation to be a beneficial strategy. In more densely connected networks, this critical mass is reached more easily.

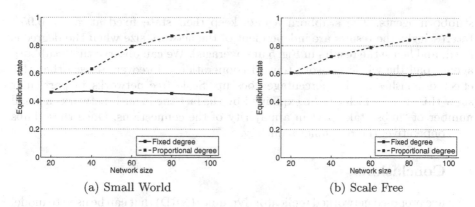

(a) Small World   (b) Scale Free

Fig. 4. The equilibrium state for different network sizes, for Small World and Scale Free networks using LF-2. Fixed degree is 2, proportional degree is 10 % of the network size.

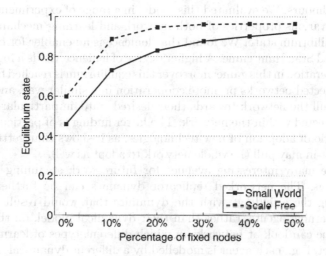

Fig. 5. The influence of the number of stubborn agents on final network state, for small world and scale free networks of degree 2.

5.4 The Influence of Stubborn Agents

Finally, we look at the influence of *stubborn agents* on the final state. Stubborn agents are ones that do not update their state, regardless of the actions of their neighbours or the rewards they receive. These agents could be perceived as regulating bodies in financial networks, or politicians in social networks trying to spread their views.

Here, we select the highest degree nodes in the network to be stubborn - future work will investigate this issue further. Figure 5 shows the results of an extensive set of experiments, simulating networks of different sizes $N \in \{20, 40, 60, 80, 100\}$ with average degree 2, and varying the percentage of stubborn agents. The stubborn agents keep their state fixed at $x_1 = 0.95$.[2] Interestingly, the results are independent of the network size when the degree is fixed, and hence the results in Fig. 5 are averaged. We can observe that stubborn agents pull the whole network toward cooperation. Moreover, we see that this effect diminishes as the percentage goes up. Scale free networks in particular show this effect, which can be explained by the fact the in such networks a small number of "hubs" take part in a majority of the connections. Once these hubs are cooperative, the rest follows quickly.

6   Conclusions

We have proposed networked replicator dynamics (NRD) that can be used to model learning in (social) networks. The model leverages the link between evolutionary game theory and multi-agent learning, that exists for unstructured populations, and extends it to settings in which agents only interact locally with their direct network neighbours. We evaluated this model in a range of experiments, showing the effect of various properties of both network and learning mechanism on the resulting equilibrium state. We found that lenience is an enabler for cooperation in a networked Stag Hunt game. A higher degree of lenience yields a higher probability of cooperation in this game; moreover this equilibrium is reached faster. More densely connected networks promote cooperation in a similar way, and stubborn agents can pull the network towards their desired state, in particular when they are well connected within the network. The latter finding is of particular interest to the scenario of adoption of new technologies, as it shows that getting few key players to opt-in may pull the whole network to adopt as well.

There are many interesting avenues for future work stemming from these initial findings. The networked replicator dynamics can be further validated by comparing these findings with the dynamics that would result from placing actual learning agents, rather than their dynamical model, on the network. Moreover, one can look at networks in which different types of learning mechanisms interact. E.g., each agent is modelled by a different dynamical model. This can be easily integrated in the NRD. Furthermore, different games can be studied as the model for various real-world scenarios, such as the N-player Stag Hunt which yields richer dynamics than its two-player counterpart [5,28]. Finally, an interesting direction for further research would be to extend the NRD model for more complex learning algorithms. For example, it has been shown that adding memory can help sustain cooperation by taking past encounters into account, e.g. by recording the opponent's intention [1] or by the inclination to stick to previous actions [13].

Acknowledgements. We thank the anonymous reviewers as well as the audience at the Artificial Life and Intelligent Agents symposium for their helpful comments and suggestions.

---

[2] Note that we exclude these fixed nodes from the results presented here, however a similar trend can be observed it they are included.

References

1. Ahn, H.T., Pereira, L.M., Santos, F.C.: Intention recognition promotes the emergence of cooperation. Adapt. Behav. **19**(4), 264–279 (2011)
2. Backstrom, L., Boldi, P., Rosa, M.: Four degrees of separation. Arxiv preprint (2011). arXiv:1111.4570
3. Barabási, A.L., Albert, R.: Emergence of scaling in random networks. Science **286**(5439), 509–512 (1999)
4. Barabási, A.L., Oltvai, Z.N.: Network biology: understanding the cell's functional organization. Nat. Rev. Genet. **5**(2), 101–113 (2004)
5. Bloembergen, D., De Jong, S., Tuyls, K.: Lenient learning in a multiplayer stag hunt. In: Proceedings of 23rd Benelux Conference on Artificial Intelligence (BNAIC 2011), pp. 44–50 (2011)
6. Bloembergen, D., Kaisers, M., Tuyls, K.: Empirical and theoretical support for lenient learning. In: Tumer, Yolum, Sonenberg, Stone (eds.) Proceedings of 10th International Conference on AAMAS 2011, pp. 1105–1106. International Foundation for AAMAS (2011)
7. Bloembergen, D., Ranjbar-Sahraei, B., Ammar, H.B., Tuyls, K., Weiss, G.: Influencing social networks: an optimal control study. In: Proceedings of the 21st ECAI 2014, pp. 105–110 (2014)
8. Börgers, T., Sarin, R.: Learning through reinforcement and replicator dynamics. J. Econ. Theor. **77**(1), 1–14 (1997)
9. Boyd, R., Gintis, H., Bowles, S.: Coordinated punishment of defectors sustains cooperation and can proliferate when rare. Science **328**(5978), 617–620 (2010)
10. Bullmore, E., Sporns, O.: Complex brain networks: graph theoretical analysis of structural and functional systems. Nat. Rev. Neurosci. **10**(3), 186–198 (2009)
11. Busoniu, L., Babuska, R., De Schutter, B.: A comprehensive survey of multiagent reinforcement learning. IEEE Trans. Syst. Man Cybern. Part C: Appl. Rev. **38**(2), 156–172 (2008)
12. Chapman, M., Tyson, G., Atkinson, K., Luck, M., McBurney, P.: Social networking and information diffusion in automated markets. In: David, E., Kiekintveld, C., Robu, V., Shehory, O., Stein, S. (eds.) AMEC 2012 and TADA 2012. LNBIP, vol. 136, pp. 1–15. Springer, Heidelberg (2013)
13. Cimini, G., Sánchez, A.: Learning dynamics explains human behaviour in prisoner's dilemma on networks. J. R. Soc. Interface **11**(94), 20131186 (2014)
14. Cross, J.G.: A stochastic learning model of economic behavior. Q. J. Econ. **87**(2), 239–266 (1973)
15. Dickens, L., Broda, K., Russo, A.: The dynamics of multi-agent reinforcement learning. In: ECAI, pp. 367–372 (2010)
16. Easley, D., Kleinberg, J.: Networks, Crowds, and Markets: Reasoning about a Highly Connected World. Cambridge University Press, Cambridge (2010)
17. Edmonds, B., Norling, E., Hales, D.: Towards the evolution of social structure. Comput. Math. Organ. Theory **15**(2), 78–94 (2009)
18. Ghanem, A.G., Vedanarayanan, S., Minai, A.A.: Agents of influence in social networks. In: Proceedings of the 11th International Conference on AAMAS 2012 (2012)
19. Han, T.A., Pereira, L.M., Santos, F.C., Lenaerts, T.: Good agreements make good friends. Sci. Rep. **3**, Article number: 2695 (2013). doi:10.1038/srep02695
20. Hofbauer, J., Sigmund, K.: Evolutionary games and population dynamics. Cambridge University Press, Cambridge (1998)

21. Hofmann, L.M., Chakraborty, N., Sycara, K.: The evolution of cooperation in self-interested agent societies: a critical study. In: Proceedings of the 10th International Conference on AAMAS 2011, pp. 685–692 (2011)
22. Jackson, M.O.: Social and Economic Networks. Princeton University Press, Princeton (2008)
23. Kaisers, M., Tuyls, K.: Frequency adjusted multi-agent Q-learning. In: Proceedings of 9th International Conference on AAMAS 2010, pp. 309–315, 10–14 May 2010
24. Maynard Smith, J., Price, G.R.: The logic of animal conflict. Nature **246**(2), 15–18 (1973)
25. Narendra, K.S., Thathachar, M.A.L.: Learning automata - a survey. IEEE Trans. Syst. Man Cybern. **4**(4), 323–334 (1974)
26. Nowak, M.A., May, R.M.: Evolutionary games and spatial chaos. Nature **359**(6398), 826–829 (1992)
27. Ohtsuki, H., Hauert, C., Lieberman, E., Nowak, M.A.: A simple rule for the evolution of cooperation on graphs and social networks. Nature **441**(7092), 502–505 (2006)
28. Pacheco, J.M., Santos, F.C., Souza, M.O., Skyrms, B.: Evolutionary dynamics of collective action in n-person stag hunt dilemmas. Proc. R. Soc. B: Biol. Sci. **276**, 315–321 (2009)
29. Panait, L., Tuyls, K., Luke, S.: Theoretical advantages of lenient learners: an evolutionary game theoretic perspective. J. Mach. Learn. Res. **9**, 423–457 (2008)
30. Ranjbar-Sahraei, B., Bou Ammar, H., Bloembergen, D., Tuyls, K., Weiss, G.: Evolution of cooperation in arbitrary complex networks. In: Proceedings of the 2014 International Conference on AAMAS 2014, pp. 677–684. International Foundation for AAMAS (2014)
31. Santos, F., Pacheco, J.: Scale-free networks provide a unifying framework for the emergence of cooperation. Phys. Rev. Lett. **95**(9), 1–4 (2005)
32. Sigmund, K., Hauert, C., Nowak, M.A.: Reward and punishment. Proc. Nat. Acad. Sci. **98**(19), 10757–10762 (2001)
33. Skyrms, B.: The Stag Hunt and the Evolution of Social Structure. Cambridge University Press, Cambridge (2004)
34. Sutton, R., Barto, A.: Reinforcement Learning: An Introduction. MIT Press, Cambridge (1998)
35. Thathachar, M., Sastry, P.S.: Varieties of learning automata: an overview. IEEE Trans. Syst. Man Cybern. Part B: Cybern. **32**(6), 711–722 (2002)
36. Tuyls, K., Verbeeck, K., Lenaerts, T.: A selection-mutation model for q-learning in multi-agent systems. In: Proceedings of 2nd International Conference on AAMAS 2003, pp. 693–700. ACM, New York (2003)
37. Ugander, J., Karrer, B., Backstrom, L., Marlow, C.: The anatomy of the facebook social graph. arXiv preprint, pp. 1–17 (2011). arXiv:1111.4503
38. Van Segbroeck, S., de Jong, S., Nowe, A., Santos, F.C., Lenaerts, T.: Learning to coordinate in complex networks. Adapt. Behav. **18**(5), 416–427 (2010)
39. Watkins, C.J.C.H., Dayan, P.: Q-learning. Mach. Learn. **8**(3), 279–292 (1992)
40. Watts, D.J., Strogatz, S.H.: Collective dynamics of 'small-world' networks. Nature **393**(6684), 440–442 (1998)
41. Weibull, J.W.: Evolutionary game theory. MIT press, Cambridge (1997)
42. Zimmermann, M.G., Eguíluz, V.M.: Cooperation, social networks, and the emergence of leadership in a prisoner's dilemma with adaptive local interactions. Phys. Rev. E **72**(5), 056118 (2005)

Human Interaction

Human Robot-Team Interaction
Towards the Factory of the Future

Daniel Claes[(⊠)] and Karl Tuyls

University of Liverpool, Ashton Building, Liverpool L69 3BX, UK
dclaes@liv.ac.uk

Abstract. In this paper we present a human robot-team interaction solution for automated task handling in an industrial work environment. The main idea is that multiple heterogenous robots with different capabilities support human workers by autonomously performing tasks for them. When a human worker asks for a specific item the robots need to collaborate as a team to grasp the item and bring it to the user. The approach combines various techniques from vision, robotics and multi-agent systems to create a flexible, low-cost solution for different task allocation problems. A proof of concept is implemented on a mobile manipulation platform and a low-cost personal robot.

1 Introduction

In the past, research in industrial robotics has largely focused on high precision and repeatability. Unfortunately, these manipulators are highly expensive w.r.t. purchase, setup and maintenance costs. Recently, the robotics and automation industry is shifting its focus towards more flexible and low-cost solutions[1]. Additionally, the integration of mobility and manipulation on a single platform has been a recent development in industry. Examples of those platforms are the KUKA youBot [4] and omniRob which are essential components of the so-called initiative for the "factory of the future (FoF)" [24].

In contrast to the well developed robotic solutions deployed in common mass-production environments, the FoF targets smaller companies in which flexible multi-purpose solutions are required, which are not yet available in industry. Example tasks are finding and acquiring parts, transportation to and from dynamic locations, assembly of simple objects etc. From these industrial goals various scientific challenges arise, i.e. perception, path planning, grasp planning, decision making, adaptability and learning, as well as challenges in multi-robot and human-robot cooperation.

The recently launched RoboCup@Work [17] competition is an initiative to stimulate research into FoF. The RoboCup@Work league (part of RoboCup [22])

---

[1] As for example the "UBR-1" from Unbounded Robotics http://unboundedrobotics. com/. and "Baxter" from Rethink Robotics http://www.rethinkrobotics.com/ baxter/.

© Springer International Publishing Switzerland 2015
C.J. Headleand et al. (Eds.): ALIA 2014, CCIS 519, pp. 61–72, 2015.
DOI: 10.1007/978-3-319-18084-7_5

directly aims at these flexible robotic solutions in work-related scenarios. Specifically, the leagues vision is to "foster research and development that enables use of innovative mobile robots equipped with advanced manipulators for current and future industrial applications, where robots cooperate with human workers for complex tasks ranging from manufacturing, automation, and parts handling up to general logistics" [23].

A shortcoming of the current RoboCup@Work competition is the limitation to one single robot for each task[2]. In this paper, we focus on this limitation and propose a distributed heterogenous robot team support system that is capable of flexibly allocating spatially distributed tasks. More specifically, we present a system in which different platforms, in this case a KUKA youBot and a Turtlebot II, perform pick and carry tasks as requested by multiple users.

The remainder of the paper is structured as follows. We start by providing the problem description in Sect. 2. We continue with necessary background in Sect. 3. Section 4 describes our approach and Sect. 5 shows an empirical proof of concept. We conclude in Sect. 6.

2 Environment and Problem Description

In this section we will present the environment and assumptions that are used for our approach. The problem we are trying to solve is described and the necessary requirements for the solution are sketched.

2.1 Environment

The environment is inspired by the RoboCup@Work arena. In the arena are several so-called service areas, i.e. tables, on which the manipulation objects can be grasped and placed. Figure 1a shows a picture of the 2013 RoboCup@Work arena and Fig. 1b shows the corresponding annotated map that is used for navigation. The manipulation objects that are used are for instance industrial nuts, bolts, aluminium profiles. Figure 2 depicts the official competition items.

In addition to the standard RoboCup arena, we assume that there are several human work spaces in the environment. The map is known and the state of the environment is fully observable, i.e. the robots and the humans can look up where each item is located. Also the robots and the humans share a common reference frame.

2.2 Problem Description

The main idea is now that the human workers can request an item to be brought to them, so that he is supported in his work and can continue with the more

---

[2] Our team smARTLab@work successfully competed in the RoboCup@Work world championships in 2013 [1] and 2014, and the German Open competitions in 2013 and 2014.

(a) (b)

Fig. 1. (a) RoboCup@Work arena with extra static obstacles. (b) Map of the arena. Annotated with service areas.

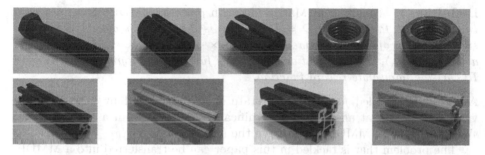

Fig. 2. Manipulation objects, from top left to bottom right: M20_100, R20, V20, M20, M30, F20_20_B, F20_20_G, S40_40_B, S40_40_G.

important tasks. In the workspace, there are multiple robots with different capabilities, i.e. only some robots can grasp and manipulate items, and other cheaper robots can transport items. These robots autonomously decide, which actions to take and plan to efficiently fulfil the tasks given by the users.

The solution should be decentralised in order to be robust against single point of failures and the planning has to be done online in order to cope with additional tasks that appear. The user needs only a simple interface to interact with the system, i.e. the necessary item has to be selected and the system takes care that the item is brought.

This setting is substantially different from other common multi-robot settings. In many cases the robots are homogeneous in type, i.e. many robots that can all perform the same task, or, if the robot team is heterogeneous, the tasks are not related or co-operative. To solve the presented problem, the robots need to be aware of the other robots' capabilities and co-operate together.

3 Background

In this section, the necessary background about planning in spatially distributed tasks and the robotic platforms that we use for our approach are described. We will give some background on Markov decision processes that can be used to deal with these kind of problems.

3.1 Planning in Spatially Distributed Tasks

Planning in cooperative multiagent systems can be neatly formalized using Multi-Agent Markov decision processes (MMDPs), but solving these models is computationally costly. The approach we follow deals with a sub-class of those MMDP problems called spatial task allocation problems (SPATAPS) that model problems in which a team of agents has to service a dynamically changing set of tasks that is spatially distributed in the environment [6].

Definition 1. *A multiagent Markov decision process (MMDP) is defined as a tuple* $\langle \mathcal{D}, \mathcal{S}, \mathcal{A}, P, R \rangle$*, where* $\mathcal{D} = \{1, \ldots, n\}$ *is the set of n agents,* $\mathcal{S}$ *a finite set of states s of the environment,* $\mathcal{A} = \mathcal{A}_1 \times \cdots \times \mathcal{A}_n$ *the set of joint actions* $a = \langle a_1, \ldots, a_n \rangle$*, T the transition probability function specifying* $P(s'|s, a)$*, and* $R(s, a)$ *the immediate reward function.*

An MMDP is called *factored* if its state space is spanned by a set of state variables. Note that an MMDP is significantly different from a Dec-MDP [3], since agents in an MMDP can observe the (global) state.

The problem that is tackled in this paper can be transferred into a MMDP, and more specifically a SPATAPS. The approximations outlined in [6] present a decentralized solution for online planning. Thus each robot observes the global state and can plan accordingly. This will be used in our approach.

3.2 Platforms

All of our robots are running the Robot Operating System (ROS) framework [21]. ROS is designed as middle-ware and framework for robotic platforms. Additionally, it is an open source toolkit to prevent "reinventing the wheel". One of the primary goals stated on the ROS website is to "support code reuse in robotics research and development"[3]. Thus, our approach is not limited to the two platforms that are presented in the following, but any robot running ROS can be adapted to work in our approach, given that it has similar capabilities.

YouBot. The youBot is an omni-directional platform that has four mecanum [14] wheels, a 5 DoF manipulator and a two finger gripper. The platform is manufactured by KUKA[4], and is commercially available at the youBot-store[5].

---

[3] For more information see: http://www.ros.org/.

[4] http://kuka.com.

[5] http://youbot-store.com/.

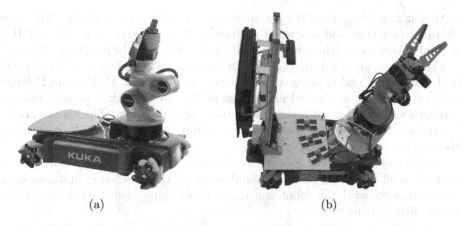

(a)   (b)

Fig. 3. (a) CAD model of a stock youBot. (b) smARTLab modified youBot.

It has been designed to work in industrial like environments and to perform various industrial tasks. With this open-source robot, KUKA is targeting educational and research markets. Figure 3a shows a model of the stock youBot.

The youBot comes with a 5-degree-of-freedom arm that is made from casted magnesium, and has a 2-degree-of-freedom gripper. The arm is 655 mm high, weighs 6.3 kg, and can handle a payload of up to 0.5 kg. The working envelope of the arm is $0.513\ m^3$, and is is connected over EtherCat [16] with the internal computer, and has a power consumption limit of 80 Watts. The gripper has two detachable fingers that can be remounted in different configurations. The gripper has a stroke of 20 mm and a reach of 50 mm, it opens and closes with an approximate speed of 1 cm/s.

In order to meet the requirements we demand from the youBot platform, we made a number of modifications to the robot. In this paragraph we describe which parts are modified and why these modifications are a necessity for our approach. Figure 3b shows the modified youBot setup. The gripper is replaced by two FESTO FinGripper fingers[6] mounted on two Dynamixel AX-12A[7] servo motors. This increases the stroke to more than 20 cm and the speed of the gripper to up to 10 cm/s. Also the fingers passively adapt to the shape of the objects.

To extend the reach of the robot-arm in respect to the chassis, we designed an extension plate of 5 mm thick aluminium. This plate can extend the arm towards the bounds of the chassis, and is designed to be a multi-purpose extension for the youBot arm. Additionally, the position of the arm is elevated by 8 cm.

For perceiving the environment, two Hokuyo URG-04LX-UG01 light detection and ranging (LIDAR) sensors are mounted parallel to the floor on the front and back of the robot.

In order to detect and recognize manipulation objects, an ASUS Xtion PRO LIVE RGBD camera is attached to the last arm joint. This camera is mounted,

---

[6] http://www.festo.com/rep/en_corp/assets/pdf/Tripod_en.pdf.

[7] http://support.robotis.com/en/product/dynamixel/ax_series/dxl_ax_actuator.htm.

so that it faces away from the manipulator, as can be seen in Fig. 5a. The main idea of this rather odd mounting position is that we want to use the RGB-D data of this camera, which is only available for distances larger than ∼0.5 m.

The base computer is upgraded from the stock ATOM based architecture to an Intel i7 CPU and is powered by a dedicated 14.8V / 5 Ah Lithium Polymer battery pack that is charged and monitored by an OpenPSU power unit. For cooling we mounted an additional fan in the base of the robot. The base computer is supported by an i5 notebook, which is mounted on a rack at the backside of the robot.

For safety reasons the robot is equipped with an emergency stop button, that stops all robot movement, without affecting the processing units, so when the stop is released the robot can continue its movement without having to re-initialize it again.

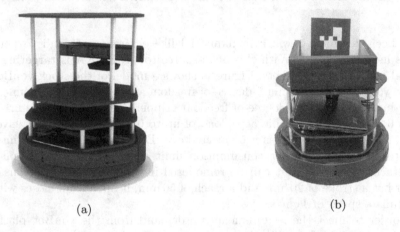

(a)   (b)

Fig. 4. (a) CAD model of a stock Turtlebot. (b) smARTLab modified Turtlebot.

Turtlebot. The Turtlebot[8] platform is a low-cost personal robot with limited resources. This robot is equipped with a laptop with core-i3 CPU for computation. We use the second generation, a Turtlebot II, for which a custom base was developed by Kobuki. As a main sensing unit the Turtlebot is originally equipped with a Microsoft Kinect RGBD sensor as shown in Fig. 4a, but in our setup it is replaced by a Hokuyo URG-04LX-UG01 light detection and ranging (LIDAR) sensor. This in order to decrease the total height of the Turtlebot, such that the items can be dropped into a carton box mounted on top of the Turtlebot. In the box, an AR marker is attached such that it can be detected by the youBot.

Figure 4b shows the final configuration. The LIDAR is mounted up side down on the top plate for protection and leaving free space for the box on top. For

---

[8] http://www.Turtlebot.com/.

static obstacle detection, we use the information of the sensor together with three bumpers that are located in the front half of the robot. Furthermore, the robot estimates its position by integrating the wheel odometry and gyro information together with the sensor readings as will be explained in more detail in the following section.

4 Approach

In this section, the different techniques used to tackle the above mentioned approach are explained. We developed different modules for many different capabilities, e.g. basic global navigation, object recognition, inverse kinematics of the arm, etc. By combining these capabilities in state-machines we are able to show a first proof of concept. The basic global navigation and marker detection modules are readily available when using ROS. However, especially the path planning needed to be heavily adapted to ensure that the robots drive efficiently. Also while the general AR marker detection is available, a further Kalman filtering step is incorporated in order to ensure a more robust detection. The inverse kinematic module and the object detection needed to be developed from scratch, since there were no ROS modules available.

Mapping and Localization. One of the most crucial capabilities of an autonomous agent is to localise itself efficiently in a known environment. To achieve this, we use gmapping [12] to build a map of the arena beforehand. The map of this years arena is shown in Fig. 1b. After the map is recorded it can be used by AMCL [10] for efficient global localization. Another solution could be to implement a "Northstar" like navigation system, by providing a fixed frame of reference which is almost always visible from any location. However, this system would be centralized and while possibly providing more accurate localization, if the "Northstar" fails, the whole system would break down.

Navigation. Another necessary capability of the robot is to navigate in the known environment without colliding with obstacles. The map created with gmapping is used for the basic global navigation. The global path is computed by an A* algorithm and is then executed using a dynamic window approach [11] trajectory roll-out for the local path planning. This planner samples different velocities and ranks them according to the distance to the goal and the distance to the path, while velocities that collide with the environment are excluded.

Object Recognition. Besides all the navigation tasks, object detection and recognition is crucial to be able to interact with the environment, i.e. picking up objects and placing them in the correct target locations. We use the openCV-library[9] to detect the objects. An adaptive threshold filter is applied to the input

---

[9] http://opencv.org.

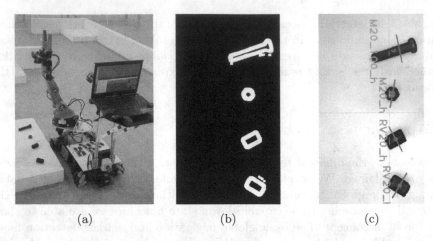

(a)   (b)   (c)

Fig. 5. (a) Pre-grip scan position. (b) Pre-processing of the image. (c) Detected objects, classification and grasp positions.

image. Afterwards the image is converted into a black and white image and this is used to detect the contours of the objects as shown in Fig. 5b. We use various features of the detected objects, e.g., length of principal axis, average intensity and area, and use a labeled data-set that we created on the location to train a J4.8 decision tree in weka [13] for the recognition of the objects. This decision tree is then used for the online classification of the objects. Figure 5c shows the detection in a service area.

(Local) Communication. Communication is realised over wi-fi with a UDP connection to each Turtlebot using the LCM library [15]. We have setup two channels, one channel is reserved for the initial global communication broadcasts, and furthermore each robot listens only to its own channel. This ensures that the communication can be initiated between any two robots, but as soon as the communication is only needed to be bidirectional between two robots, the broadcast channel does not get flooded with messages.

Inverse Kinematics of the Arm. In order to manipulate the detected objects, the various joints of the arm have to be controlled such that the objects are grasped correctly. We implemented a simple inverse kinematics [20] module to calculate the joint values for any top-down gripping point that is in the reach of the robot. Since we are gripping from a top-down position, the inverse kinematics can be solved exactly, when we fix the first joint such that it is always pointing in the direction of the gripping point as shown in Fig. 6. Then the remaining joints can be calculated in a straight forward manner, by solving the angles of a triangle with three known side lengths, since we know the distance of the grip and also the lengths of all the arm-segments. Since the position-reproducibility

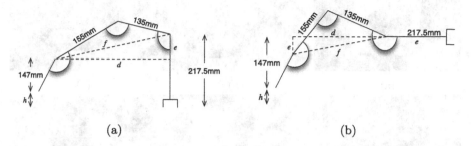

(a)   (b)

Fig. 6. Simple inverse kinematics: d and h are the grip distance and height, relative to the mount point of the arm. By always gripping from a top down position (a) or vertical position (b), e and f can be calculated and by that we can determine all angles for the joints.

of the arm is in sub millimetre order, this proved to be sufficient for performing highly accurate grasp and place trajectories.

Marker Detection. To enable visual robot-robot detection between the Turtlebot and the youBot, we equipped the Turtlebot with a AR marker. This is oriented in a way that it is visible when the two robots are facing each other. To track and decode these markers we make use of a toolkit called ALVAR, more specifically we use the ROS wrapper[10] of this library. The youBot uses the camera on the arm to search for the marker and then it can use the marker's position to calculate the inverse kinematics for dropping an object in the box attached on top of the Turtlebot.

5   Proof of Concept

We implemented a first proof of concept on a Turtlebot II and a youBot. A video about the approach can be found here: http://youtu.be/II1QEvvkvHg. Figure 7 summarizes the steps implemented in the system.

The user selects an item that is needed using a simple touch interface. The request is translated to a task and broadcast to the system. In the task description, the target location and the item are specified. The youBot looks up where the item is located and drives to the target location[11]. The youBot searches the item on the source platform and broadcasts a pick-up task to the system. As soon as a Turtlebot confirms the pick-up, the item is grasped, while the Turtlebot drives to the source platform in front of the youBot. The Turtlebot notifies the youBot that it has arrived. The youBot searches for the marker on top of the Turtlebot to be able to drop the item into the box. Inverse kinematics are

---

[10] http://wiki.ros.org/ar_track_alvar.
[11] Due to a damaged motor and wheel, the youBot is stationary at the moment.

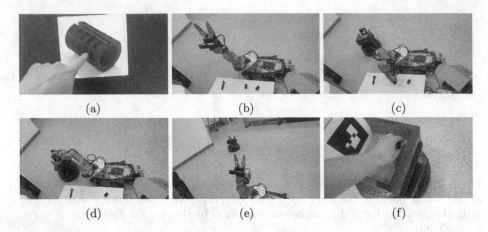

Fig. 7. (a) The user selects an item. (b) The youBot scans the platform and notifies the Turtlebot that the item is found. (c) The item is grasped while the Turtlebot is approaching. (d) The item is placed in the bin ontop of the Turtlebot. (e) The item is transported back to the user. (f) The user can take the item.

applied in order to compensate for the location of the Turtlebot. After the item is placed in the box, the youBot notifies the Turtlebot, so that it can leave and bring the item to the target destination. When the Turtlebot has arrived at the user's location, the item can be picked up out of the box and the robots become free to select the next task.

At the moment, the online planning is very limited, since there is only one Turtlebot and one youBot in the system. However as soon as the system is extended to more robots and humans, the online planning mechanism becomes a major part of the system.

6   Conclusions and Future Work

This paper investigates human team-robot coordination in a factory of the future setting. It presents a proof-of-concept of an approach based on the combination of basic global navigation, object recognition, inverse kinematics and human-robot interaction. A conceptual overview is presented of our human robot-team interaction solution. Our initial experiment shows the feasibility of the approach.

In the future, the system will be extended to more robots with multiple tasks that have to be serviced at the same time. We also aim to introduce time constraints, such as for instance an item has to be delivered within a certain time-frame. As soon as many robots share a common workspace, a good and efficient collision avoidance system is necessary. We intend to implement a solution based on the approach explained in [5]. The advantage of this solution is that it can also be completely decentralized and does only rely on robot-robot detection.

Additionally, the approach enables to compare different strategies for allocating the tasks. For instance it would be very insightful to compare the SPATAPS

approach with a greedy approach and solution based on bidding and auctioning for the tasks. Lastly, the approaches can be compared with nature inspired
algorithms such as from ants [7] and bees [8,9,19]. These approaches rely on
indirect communication based on pheromone trails, or more recently also non
pheromone-based approaches have been developed as in [2,18]. An interesting
research direction would be to compare the swarm-based approaches with the
approaches mentioned before based on planning and/or auctioning.

References

1. Alers, S., Claes, D., Fossel, J., Hennes, D., Tuyls, K., Weiss, G.: How to win
   RoboCup@Work? In: Behnke, S., Veloso, M., Visser, A., Xiong, R. (eds.) RoboCup
   2013. LNCS, vol. 8371, pp. 147–158. Springer, Heidelberg (2014)
2. Alers, S., Tuyls, K., Ranjbar-Sahraei, B., Claes, D., Weiss, G.: Insect-inspired robot
   coordination: foraging and coverage. In: The Fourteenth Conference on the Synthesis and Simulation of Living Systems (ALIFE) (2014)
3. Bernstein, D.S., Givan, R., Immerman, N., Zilberstein, S.: The complexity of decentralized control of Markov decision processes. Math. Oper. Res. **27**(4), 819–840
   (2002)
4. Bischoff, R., Huggenberger, U., Prassler, E.: Kuka youbot - a mobile manipulator
   for research and education. In: 2011 IEEE International Conference on Robotics
   and Automation (ICRA), pp. 1–4, May 2011
5. Claes, D., Hennes, D., Tuyls, K., Meeussen, W.: Collision avoidance under bounded
   localization uncertainty. In: Proceedings of IEEE/RSJ International Conference on
   Intelligent Robots and Systems (IROS 2012), Vilamoura, Portugal, October 2012
6. Claes, D., Robbel, P., Oliehoek, F.A., Hennes, D., Tuyls, K.: Effective Approximations for Spatial Task Allocation Problems. In: Proceedings of the 25th Benelux
   Conference on Artifical Intelligence (BNAIC) (2013)
7. Dorigo, M., Birattari, M., Stutzle, T.: Ant colony optimization: artificial ants as
   a computational intelligence technique. IEEEComput. Intell. Mag. **1**(4), 28–39
   (2006)
8. Dressler, F., Akan, O.B.: A survey on bio-inspired networking. Comput. Net. **54**(6),
   881–900 (2010)
9. Floreano, D., Mattiussi, C.: Bio-Inspired Artificial Intelligence: Theories, Methods,
   and Technologies. The MIT Press, Cambridge (2008)
10. Fox, D., Burgard, W., D., F., Thrun, S.: Monte carlo localization: efficient position
    estimation for mobile robots. In: Proceedings of the Sixteenth National Conference
    on Artificial Intelligence (AAAI 1999) (1999)
11. Fox, D., Burgard, W., Thrun, S.: The dynamic window approach to collision avoid-
    ance. In: IEEERobotics & Automation Magazine, vol. 4 (1997)
12. Grisetti, G., Stachniss, C., Burgard, W.: Improved techniques for grid mapping
    with rao-blackwellized particle filters. IEEE Trans. Rob. **23**, 43–46 (2007)
13. Hall, M., Eibe, F., Holmes, G., Pfahringer, B., Reutemann, P., Witten, I.H.: The
    weka data mining software: an update. SIGKDD Explor. Newsl. **11**(1), 10–18
    (2009)
14. Hon, B.E.: Wheels for a course stable selfpropelling vehicle movable in any desired
    direction on the ground or some other base, U.S. Patent 3,876,255 (1975)

15. Huang, A., Olson, E., Moore, D.: LCM: lightweight communications and marshalling. In: Proceedings of the IEEE/RSJ International Conference on Intelligent Robots and Systems (IROS), pp. 4057–4062, October 2010
16. Jansen, D., Buttner, H.: Real-time ethernet: the ethercat solution. Comput. Control Eng. **15**(1), 16–21 (2004)
17. Kraetzschmar, G.K., Hochgeschwender, N., Nowak, W., Hegger, F., Schneider, S., Dwiputra, R., Berghofer, J., Bischoff, R.: RoboCup@Work: competing for the factory of the future. In: Bianchi, R.A.C., Akin, H.L., Ramamoorthy, S., Sugiura, K. (eds.) RoboCup 2014. LNCS, vol. 8992, pp. 171–182. Springer, Heidelberg (2015)
18. Lemmens, N.: Bee-inspired Distributed Optimization. Maastricht University, Maastricht (2011)
19. Lemmens, N., Tuyls, K.: Stigmergic landmark optimization. Adv. Complex Syst. **15**(8), 1150025-1–1150025-41 (2012). http://www.worldscientific.com/doi/abs/10.1142/S0219525911500251
20. McCarthy, J.: An Introduction to Theoretical Kinematics Mass. MIT Press, Cambridge (1990)
21. Quigley, M., Gerkey, B., Conley, K., Faust, J., Foote, T., Leibs, J., Berger, E., Wheeler, R., Ng, A.Y.: ROS: An open-source Robot Operating System. In: Proceedings of the Open-Source Software Workshop (ICRA) (2009)
22. RoboCup: RoboCup (2013). http://www.robocup.org/
23. RoboCup@Work: RoboCup@Work (2013). http://www.robocupatwork.org/
24. TAPAS Project: Robotics-enabled Logistics and Assistive Services for the Transformable Factory of the Future (TAPAS) (2013). http://tapas-project.eu/

An Exploration on Intuitive Interfaces for Robot Control Based on Self Organisation

Christos Melidis[✉] and Davide Marocco

School of Computing and Mathematics, Plymouth University, Plymouth, UK
{christos.melidis,davide.marocco}@plymouth.ac.uk

Abstract. In this paper we present the results of a preliminary study on behaviour extraction from arbitrary robotic morphologies. Our goal is to build a universal interface targeting all possible robotic morphologies. For the exploration of the capabilities of different morphologies, we focus on the self organisation of the sensorimotor loop for discovering behavioural capabilities. In this paper we briefly explain the core idea for such an interface and present preliminary results of our method together with future remarks.

Keywords: Robotics · Self organisation · Operator behaviour acquisition

1 Introduction

The remote control of mechanical devices equipped with a large number of actuators, such as humanoid robots, is a challenging task. When dealing with the resulting large number of degrees-of-freedom, the nature of the interface provided to the human operator plays a fundamental role in the success of tele-robotic performance. A wide range of tele-robotic interfaces have been explored so far; some are very rigid devices that require a great deal of cognitive and manual effort, while other more intuitive systems, based on one-to-one body mapping, are in contrast very complex and expensive devices, often specifically tailored to a single robotic platform [3].

Our goal is the implementation of an agile interface able to control every possible robotic morphology, a universal interface. To do so we need an automated mechanism that can examine and explore the robotic morphology connected to the interface and extract interesting features, with respect to the desired control pattern. Our interest in this preliminary study is movement control. We identify interesting features as behaviours that can be produced by the robot and are meaningful to the user, according to the task in hand. The purpose of the interface is to map the behaviours of the operator to those produced by the robots, resulting in the association between the robots and operator behaviours. In order to achieve this, we reverse the informational flow of the interface, as suggested in [6]. The robot acts first and the operator responds to the exhibited behaviour with his own, through the input device. The input device thus, plays

© Springer International Publishing Switzerland 2015
C.J. Headleand et al. (Eds.): ALIA 2014, CCIS 519, pp. 73–79, 2015.
DOI: 10.1007/978-3-319-18084-7_6

a critical part on the behaviours the operator can have. Multidimensional input devices, i.e. Kinect sensor, could enable a whole body mapping, whereas simpler ones, i.e. on-off switches or joysticks, are more restrictive [2,8,9].

The interface is able to explore the capabilities of the robotic morphology based on the homeokinesis principle [1]. As described by Martius and colleagues in [5], self organisation of the sensorimotor loop can explore the behavioural repertoire of a robot. Based on this research we formulate the principles for the interaction between the interface and the robot. For the interaction between the interface and the human operator we propose a framework for a behaviour based interaction, though currently only capable of exhibiting a simple example of such interaction. In this study, we explore the applicability of the proposed method for behavioural exploration of the robotic morphology.

1.1 Operator Behaviour Acquisition

In this section we describe the main ideas guiding the interaction of the operator with the interface. As previously stated, the overall goal is to build a novel interface that connects intuitive human behaviours to robotics ones. Our approach follows the research described in [6]. In their approach they define the interaction between the user and the interface as an "intention translation" mechanism, by which user intentions are translated to instructions or commands that the interface can understand, so that the user can interact with it. In most interfaces users have to familiarise themselves with the interface in order to interact with it, read the user manual and understand the predefined mechanisms of interaction [4]. In a more complex interaction paradigm, where the actions to be performed are formed using simpler actions as building blocks, the user has to learn sequences of controls in order to communicate their intentions to the interface. In such case, as the number of sequences, and so, the building blocks increase, the more laborious it becomes for the user to remember and execute them.

Providing a mapping between user intentions and robot behaviours can lead to an intuitive interface. The operator's intentions are taken into account - through the manipulation of the input device- making the interfacing process easier and more personalised. In this reversed paradigm, users do not have to familiarise themselves with the interface, but the interface can learn from the interaction with the user. Based on the reactions of the user to the exhibited behaviours of the robot, the interface is able to correlate the two, forming a control pattern. For that to happen, a level of consistency is expected from the users in the behaviours they exhibit. Same or similar input signals should be expected to yield the same robot behaviour as a response. Studies carried out, on a similar approach show up to 80 % percent mapping accuracy in the interaction with a 17 degree of freedom robot, using an input device consisting of two joysticks [6].

2   Materials and Methods

Based on the principles explained in the introduction, we implemented a system consisting of two modules. One used for the exploration and self organisation of the sensorimotor loop of the robot and one for the extraction, storage and reuse of the acquired behaviours. The robotic morphologies used for the experiments described in this paper where simulated by the Open Dynamics Engine, ODE [7]. The module for the self organisation of the sensorimotor loop was implemented according to the system described in [5] and follows a dynamical system app-roach. The realization of the dynamics of the robot and the world is done using a Controller (K) and World Model (W) cooperating for the effective exploration of the robots dynamics and an accurate prediction of world states, respectively. Both are described by the equations bescribed below.

The exploration module, in general, is described, according to time t, as:

$$\tilde{\mathbf{x}}_{t+1} = W(K(\mathbf{x}_t, C), A) \tag{1}$$

The controller K generates motor outputs $\mathbf{y}_t = K(\mathbf{x}_t, C)$ as a function of sensory inputs $\mathbf{x} = x_1, x_2, \ldots, x_n$, in dependence on a set of parameters defined by the matrix $C_{n,n+1}$ and is defined by the equation:

$$K = g(\sum_{i=1}^{n} C_i x_i + C_{n+1}), \tag{2}$$

where g is a sigmoid function.

The world model $\tilde{\mathbf{x}}_{t+1} = W(\mathbf{y}_t, A)$ estimates future sensory inputs $\tilde{\mathbf{x}}_{t+1}$ from motor outputs $\mathbf{y}_t = y_1, y_2, \ldots, y_n$ in dependence on a set of parameters defined by the matrix $A_{n,n+1}$.

The parameter matrix of the world model, A, is adapted according to the Widrow - Hoff Learning Rule [10], delta rule, $\Delta w = +\eta E_W \mathbf{x}$ with the error, E_W, described by the function:

$$E_W = ||\mathbf{x}_{t+1} - \tilde{\mathbf{x}}_{t+1}||^2 \tag{3}$$

with learning rate $\eta = 0.1$.

The controller updates its parameter matrix by gradient descent with respect to the error function,

$$E_K = ||\mathbf{x}_t - \tilde{\mathbf{x}}_t||^2 \tag{4}$$

To calculate the above error, we find the $\tilde{\mathbf{x}}_t$ by calculating the motor input $\hat{\mathbf{y}}_t$ the world model should have in order to make a perfect prediction and then the sensory input the controller K should have to predict the motor output $\tilde{\mathbf{y}}_t$. The update on the controller parameter follows the rule $C_{t+1} = C_t - \epsilon \frac{\partial E_K}{C}$, with a learning rate $\epsilon = 0.01$.

For the identification, storage and reuse of the different behaviours exhibited by the robot, we use a series of m neural networks. Each network is defined according to the equation,

$$(\mathbf{x}_{t+1}, \mathbf{y}_t) = N_i(\mathbf{x}_t, \mathbf{x}_{t-1}), \quad i = 1, \ldots, m \tag{5}$$

The neural networks, working in parallel, compete for the prediction of the motor command $\mathbf{y}_t$ of time t and the sensory input $\mathbf{x}_{t+1}$ of the next time step. It is a winner takes it all method, with only the winning network being allowed to train on the current data $\mathbf{x}_t$ and $\mathbf{x}_{t-1}$. Because of that, each network specializes to a region of the possible motoric and sensory space.

The networks consist of 3 layers, input, output and a hidden layer. The hidden layer consists of sigmoid units whereas the input and output layers from linear units. No bias units are introduced in the networks.

The algorithm for the training of the networks is backpropagation, with learning rate $\eta = 0.01$. In each time step all the networks are activated with the same input and the one with the best approximation of the next sensor values and motor commands is selected as the winning network. The sample won is then added to the training dataset of the winning network and it is trained for another epoch. For the selection of network, a smoothed error is used, taking into account the past errors of the network.

3   Results

In this section we present the experimental results of the exploration method and the way by which the interface controls the different behaviours extracted. For testing purposes we applied the method to three different robotic morphologies as seen in Fig. 1, with varying degrees of freedom and numbers of joints. The acrobot has 1; Fig. 1(a), the octacrawl has 2; Fig. 1(b) and the arm has 18; shoulder, elbow and wrist pitch together with finger pitch for three joints in every finger, Fig. 1(c). In Fig. 2 we can see how the experts are trained to identify different sensor states. Here, only a couple of behaviours extracted from the octacrawl morphology are displayed. As we can see from the graph, the outputs of the network, describing each behaviour -as captured by the sensor values- stabilize and approximate the real ones more accurately as time and training size increment. In the example of Fig. 2, behaviour 1 stabilizes faster that behaviour 2 as we can see from the convergence to a finite set of sensor values for each behaviour. This is caused by the difference in the size of the datasets for each behaviour. Some behaviours are more frequent than others making the dataset of the network describing them to increase in size faster than others. We can also observe a periodicity in the

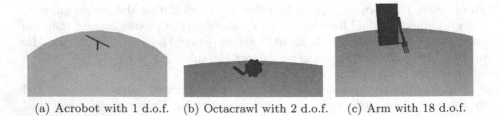

(a) Acrobot with 1 d.o.f.   (b) Octacrawl with 2 d.o.f.   (c) Arm with 18 d.o.f.

Fig. 1. The different robotic morphologies used during the experiments

sensory values recorded, a direct result of the dynamical system approach used in the exploration mechanism. A behaviour is usually found when the system enters a basin of attraction, and a long-time behaviour is exhibited by the system as it approaches the attraction point.

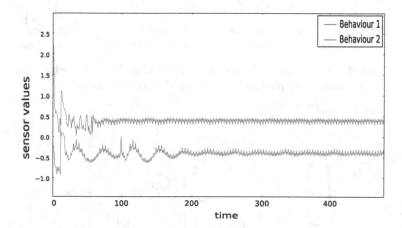

Fig. 2. Plot of the sensor values for two different behaviours extracted from the octacrawl morphology, as they change through time during the learning phase

Even more interesting features of the system can be observed in the switching between behaviours. In Fig. 3(a) the behavioural changes of the acrobot morphology are being displayed against time. The different behaviours become salient by the different sensor readings they produce. In Fig. 3(c) and (b) the behaviours of the octacrawl morphology and the arm morphology are being displayed against time, respectively. Our interest in these graphs lies in the point of change between behaviours. We exhibit a behaviour by activating the corresponding network. The id of the active network is noted in the horizontal axis, above time. For the rest of this section, behavioural change results from the change of network in charge. So, whenever a behavioural change is stated, the reader should keep in mind that the network in charge has changed in order to support the different dynamics dictated by the behaviour.

In all cases the exploration mechanism was able to identify and extract different behaviours. Theses behaviours where triggered through the interface in random order and the sensor values of each morphology were recorded and predicted by the network in control. In all graphs of the Fig. 3 we observe smooth changes in the sensory recordings, regardless of the changes in behaviours. The system, readjusts itself, following a trajectory to the new attractor, described by the network in control each instant. In the first time steps following a behavioural change, we can observe the readjustment of the morphology, as recorded through the sensor values, so as to exhibit the desired behaviour.

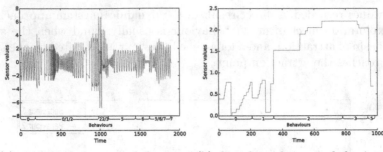

(a) Switching between behaviours using the acrobot morphology

(b) Switching between behaviours using the arm morphology

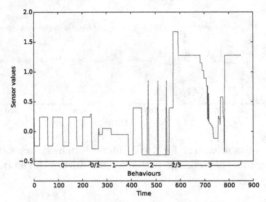

(c) Switching between behaviours using the octacrawl morphology

Fig. 3. Switching between behaviours in the different morphologies used. In the horizontal axis we have time, and the id of the expert(s) at control of the system. The expert id is displayed and when two or more experts are in control at the same time, their ids are separated with '/'. In the vertical axis the sensor values of the each robot are being displayed.

At the same graphs of Fig. 3 we can also observe the behaviour of the system in the case of simultaneous activations. In the horizontal axis we can see the behaviours exhibited by the morphology, separated with '/' when more than one behaviours are triggered. In the co-activation of behaviours we have the ability through the interface to adjust the level in which each behaviour contributes to the resulting one. The behaviours displayed in the graphs have been equally contributing to the behaviour exhibited, but experiments with different levels of contribution yield similar results. From the graphs we can see the ability of the system to mix the behaviours acquired seamlessly with no abnormal sensory readings or resulting behaviours being exhibited by the morphology. In Fig. 3(a) and (c) we observe the change in sensor values through time for the acrobot and octacrawl morphologies respectively.

4   Conclusions

In this preliminary study of the proposed interfacing mechanism we were able to show that the proposed exploration mechanism for robot behaviours was successfully implemented. The robustness of the proposed mechanism was shown, both by the stability of the mechanism when switching between the explored behaviours, and by the ability of the explored behaviours to be combined together, potentially exhibiting more complex behaviours. The next step, will be the implementation of an interface based on the proposed interfacing principles, able to support continuous interaction with the user. Once the user is able to provide continuous feedback based on the robots behaviour, we could use that to guide the exploration of the behaviours towards desired ones, depending on the task. On the exploratory mechanism, a proposed extension would be the reuse of the extracted behaviours inside the self organising mechanism so as to guide the exploration towards more complex and fine grained behaviours. In this case the user could be the one deciding which behaviours should be extended and which not, tailoring the interface system according to their needs.

References

1. Der, R.: Selforganized robot behavior from the principle of homeokinesis. In: Proceedings of the Workhop Soave, pp. 39–46 (2000)
2. Fong, T., Thorpe, C.: Vehicle teleoperation interfaces. Auton. Rob. **11**(1), 9–18 (2001)
3. Gonzalez, B., Carroll, E., Latulipe, C.: Dance-inspired technology, technology-inspired dance. In: Proceedings of the 7th Nordic Conference on Human-Computer Interaction: Making Sense Through Design, pp. 398–407. ACM (2012)
4. Kadous, M.W., Sheh, R.K.M., Sammut, C.: Effective user interface design for rescue robotics. In: Proceedings of the 1st ACM SIGCHI/SIGART Conference on Human-Robot Interaction, pp. 250–257. ACM (2006)
5. Martius, G., Fiedler, K., Herrmann, J.M.: Structure from behavior in autonomous agents. In: IEEE/RSJ International Conference on Intelligent Robots and Systems, IROS 2008, pp. 858–862. IEEE (2008)
6. Niwa, M., Okada, S., Sakaguchi, S., Azuma, K., Iizuka, H., Ando, H., Maeda, T.: Detection and transmission of "tsumori": an archetype of behavioral intention in controlling a humanoid robot. In: Proceeding of 20th International Conference on Artificial Reality and Telexistance (ICAT 2010), pp. 197–201 (2010)
7. Smith, R., et al.: Open dynamics engine (2005)
8. Watanabe, K., Yoneda, Y.: The world's smallest biped humanoid robot i-sobot. In: 2009 IEEE Workshop on Advanced Robotics and its Social Impacts (ARSO), pp. 51–53. IEEE (2009)
9. Watanabe, K., Kawabuchi, I., Kawakami, N., Maeda, T., Tachi, S.: Torso: development of a telexistence visual system using a 6-dof robot head. Adv. Rob. **22**(10), 1053–1073 (2008)
10. Widrow, B., Hoff jr., M.E., et al.: Adaptive switching circuits. IRE WESCON Convention Record **4**, 96–104 (1960)

Adaptive Training for Aggression de-Escalation

Tibor Bosse[1(✉)], Charlotte Gerritsen[2], Jeroen de Man[1],
and Suzanne Tolmeijer[1]

[1] Department of Computer Science, Vrije Universiteit Amsterdam,
De Boelelaan 1081a, 1081 HV Amsterdam, The Netherlands
{t.bosse,j.de.man}@vu.nl, suzanne.tolmeijer@gmail.com
[2] Netherlands Institute for the Study of Crime and Law Enforcement,
De Boelelaan 1077a, 1081 HV Amsterdam, The Netherlands
cgerritsen@nscr.nl

Abstract. The ability to de-escalate confrontations with aggressive individuals is a useful skill, in particular within professions in public domains. Nevertheless, offering appropriate training that enables students to develop such skills is a nontrivial matter. As a complementary approach to real-world training, the STRESS project proposes a simulation-based environment for training of aggression de-escalation. The main focus of the current paper is to make this system adaptive to the performance of the trainee. To realize this, first a number of learning goals have been identified. Based on these, several levels of difficulty were established, as well as a mechanism to switch up and down between these levels based on the user's score. A preliminary evaluation demonstrated that the system successfully adapts its difficulty level to the performance of the user, and that users are generally positive about the adaptation mechanism.

Keywords: Virtual reality · Adaptive training · Human-agent interaction

1 Introduction

People working in the public sector (e.g. police officers, ambulance personnel, public transport employees) are often confronted with aggressive behavior. According to a recent study, around 60 % of the employees in the public sector in the Netherlands have been confronted with such behavior in the last 12 months [1]. Being confronted with (verbal) aggression can have severe consequences and is closely associated with psychological distress, which in turn can have a negative impact on work performance [2]. Responses to aggression range from emotions like anger and humiliation through intent to leave the profession, and verbal aggression by customers may even impair employees' recognition and working memory [3]. In case of extreme incidents, employees may even develop symptoms indicating post-traumatic stress syndrome [4].

To deal with aggression, a variety of techniques are available that may prevent escalation [5, 6]. These include communication skills (both verbal and non-verbal), conflict resolution strategies, and emotion regulation techniques. The current paper is part of a project (called STRESS [7]) that aims to develop a serious game [8] for

© Springer International Publishing Switzerland 2015
C.J. Headleand et al. (Eds.): ALIA 2014, CCIS 519, pp. 80–93, 2015.
DOI: 10.1007/978-3-319-18084-7_7

aggression de-escalation training, based on Virtual Reality. VR-based training has proven to be a cost-effective alternative for real world training in a variety of domains, including military missions [9], surgery [10] and negotiation [11].

The core of the STRESS project is the development of an intelligent training system that is able to analyze the behavior of human trainees while they interact with aggressive virtual agents. Users of the system will be placed in front of a 3D Virtual Reality (VR) environment (see Fig. 1) that is either projected on a computer screen or on a head-mounted display. During the training, users will be placed in a virtual scenario in a particular domain (e.g., issuing parking tickets, or selling tram tickets), which involves one or more virtual agents that at some point in time start behaving aggressively (e.g., insulting the tram driver because he is late). The user's task is to de-escalate the aggressive behavior of the virtual agents by applying the appropriate communication techniques. Users will be able to communicate with the agents via multiple modalities (e.g., text, speech, facial expression). Meanwhile, they will be monitored by intelligent software that observes and analyzes the behavior and physiological state (e.g., heart rate, skin conductance, brain activity) of the trainee and provides tailored feedback [12, 13].

Fig. 1. Screenshot of the VR environment used in the STRESS project (The VR environment has been developed by IC3D Media (www.ic3dmedia.com)).

Feedback will consist of two categories, namely hints and prompts on the one hand, and run-time modification in the scenarios on the other hand. An example of the former would be to inform the trainee that (s)he should use a more empathic communication style, whereas an example of the latter would be to decrease the difficulty level in case the trainee makes many mistakes. In order to offer this feedback in a personalized manner, it is very important that the system *adapts* it to the needs of individual users. Adapting a task to the behavior of the trainee is a well-known training paradigm in a variety of domains. Hence, the current paper presents a mechanism for adaptive training of aggression de-escalation. The emphasis is on adapting the difficulty level of the scenarios offered to the performance of the trainee.

The remainder of this paper is organized as follows. In Sect. 2, the existing literature on aggression is discussed, as well as the prescribed approaches to de-escalate aggression. In Sect. 3, the state-of-the-art on adaptive training is reviewed. Next, a conceptual model for adaptive training and its implementation are presented in Sects. 4 and 5, followed by some preliminary results in Sect. 6. In Sect. 7, the paper is concluded with a discussion.

2 Aggression de-Escalation

Within psychological literature, a distinction is made between two important theories regarding the nature of aggression: aggression can be either *functional* (or *proactive*) or *emotional* (or *reactive*). One of the key differences between these two types is the absence or presence of anger [14].

When the aggression is of a functional nature, the aggressive behavior is not a response to some negative event, but is used instrumentally to achieve a goal. The *social learning theory* states that aggressive behavior can be learned through positive reinforcement [15]. The essence of this theory is that if a person has used aggression to achieve a goal in the past, and if this behavior was successful, then by operant conditioning (s)he will be likely to follow the same behavioral pattern in the future.

In contrast with functional aggression, aggression can also have an emotional nature, meaning that it is an angry reaction to a negative event that frustrates a person's desires. The *frustration-aggression hypothesis* [16] tells us that aggression flows forth from a person's goals being frustrated. Such a person is likely to be angry with respect to whatever stopped him from achieving his goal. By a carry-over effect, the anger can be transferred to new situations as well [17].

To de-escalate aggressive behavior, it is important that public service workers understand the specific type of aggression they are dealing with, as each type of aggression requires a different approach. In particular, in situations when dealing with a functional aggressor, a *directive* type of intervention is assumed to be most effective, focusing on an alteration of the contingencies associated with the aggression. In this case it is necessary to show the aggressor that there is a limit to how far he can pursue his aggressive behavior, and making him aware of the consequences of this behavior. Instead, when dealing with an emotional aggressor, more *supportive* behavior from the de-escalator is required, for example by ignoring the conflict-seeking behavior, making contact with the aggressor and actively listening to what he has to say. According to [18], such interventions should focus on reducing hostile attribution biases, i.e., the tendency to perceive others as threatening.

This distinction between functional and emotional aggression, as well as the associated de-escalation techniques (i.e., directive vs. supportive approaches), are some of the key assumptions underlying the training system developed in the STRESS project. The following sections will present a mechanism to train the relevant communication skills in an adaptive manner.

3 Adaptive Training

Adapting the difficulty level of a task to the performance of the player has been a well-known paradigm in serious gaming (and learning in general) for many years. The main underlying idea is that players' learning experience is related to their level of *motivation*. In general, if an activity is more engaging, interesting and engrossing, motivation will be higher [19]. However, this does not always imply that the difficulty level of a certain task should be maximal. Instead, especially when it comes to digital games, there are also situations in which motivation can be increased by lowering the difficulty level. Van den Hoogen and colleagues describe the relation between a difficulty level and a player's mental state as follows: '*Through striking the balance between a person's skills and the challenges an activity offers, that person may arrive in a psychological state known as flow. [...] Flow may gradually increase over the course of the game in a homeostatic positive feedback loop, until either the challenge becomes too great (resulting in frustration) or the player's skill outpaces the challenges the game can offer (leading to boredom)*' [20]. This suggests that there exists something like an optimal level of difficulty (or challenge) that yields maximal learning experience, which is often used as an argument to develop flexible training games that adapt dynamically to the player's behavior.

Indeed, the recent literature shows a number of examples of such adaptive training systems, which in one way or another tune their internal parameters to the user's state or behavior. For example, Holmes et al. [21] have demonstrated that adaptive training may be used to overcome learning difficulties for people with impairments in working memory. Wickens et al. [22] have shown 'increasing difficulty' to be a successful technique in knowledge transfer when implemented adaptively (but not when increased in fixed steps). Also, several authors focus on increasing players' affective experience by adapting the emotional content of a game; see, e.g., [23]. Finally, Yannakakis et al. [24] argue that adaptive serious gaming is an effective method for training of conflict resolution skills. Unlike the current paper, they focus on children as their user group, rather than on security personnel. An overview of design principles to develop effective adaptive training systems is provided in [25].

4 Conceptual Model

In this section, the proposed model for adaptive training is described at a conceptual level. First, a number of relevant learning goals are formulated. After that, the structure of the model is described, based on the notion of dialog system. Finally, the idea of difficulty levels is introduced, as well as a mechanism to switch between them.

4.1 Learning Goals

As mentioned in the introduction, the main learning goal of the proposed system is to be able to de-escalate confrontations with (verbally) aggressive individuals, in order to prevent these individuals from becoming physically aggressive. Based on discussions with domain experts, the following sub-goals have been identified:

- *Recognizing the type of aggression*: are we dealing with a person that is showing emotional or functional aggression? To assess this, trainees need to observe the verbal as well as the non-verbal behavior of the aggressive individual. In general, emotionally aggressive people will show more arousal (e.g., flushed face, emotional speech) than functionally aggressive people. Also, the context should be taken into account (e.g., someone who just finds out that he lost his ticket will be more emotional that someone who knew this all along, and just tries to intimidate the tram driver to ride for free).

- *Selecting the appropriate response*: based on the type of aggression observed, the trainee needs to either show some empathy (in case of emotional aggression) or act more dominantly (in case of functional aggression). It is crucial for the training that these responses are not swapped; in other words, showing empathy is case of functional aggression, or acting dominantly in case of emotional aggression is undesired.
- *Being able to make decisions under time pressure*: after some practice, the trainee should be able to perform the tasks mentioned above within limited time, and without much cognitive effort.

4.2   Structure

To train users to acquire the above skills, the STRESS project works with a dialog system where users (playing the role of the public service worker) engage in a conversation with a virtual agent (playing the role of a difficult customer). Conversations are represented as simple decision trees where user and virtual agent exchange sentences according to a turn-taking protocol. In this paper, the conversations used are text-based only and consist of a short introduction, the latest response of the customer and a multiple-choice list of possible answers.[1] In the remainder of this paper, we will refer to this as a *question*, to which the trainee has to choose the most appropriate response considering the situation. An example of a question in the context of aggression de-escalation training for tram drivers is the following, taken from [26]:

'A passenger enters the tram and wants to check in, but the balance on his public transport card turns out to be insufficient. You tell him that his balance is too low to check in. The passenger reacts with surprise, and says: *No, are you kidding me?! Really?! O my god, something should have went wrong with those damn machines of yours! Can't you for once just take me with you? I am in an extreme hurry!* What do you respond?'

a. I'm sorry sir, I feel really bad for you. But don't worry, you can just buy a ticket from me. Or if you prefer, you quickly run to the machine; over there you can recharge your card in a second!
b. Too bad sir, our policy states that we only take paying customers on board. There is no other option for you than to buy a ticket or leave the tram.
c. Sir, that's the way it is, these are the rules. You will have to but a new ticket.'

Note that this example addresses a case of emotional aggression, where the customer shows clear signs of emotional arousal (most notably swearing), probably caused

---

[1] Nevertheless, the project as a whole also explores other interaction modalities, such as speech, facial expressions and gestures.

by the unexpected message that his balance is too low. In such cases, the most appropriate way to respond would be by showing empathy and offering potential solutions for the problem: this is represented by answer (a). The other two answers, (b) and (c), have an increasingly dominant (and less empathic) tone, which makes them the less appropriate responses in this type of situation.

For each question, a database with potential answers is established (although during training only a few of them (e.g., three) are offered in the multiple-choice menu). To enable the system to assess automatically which answers should be considered as appropriate, for each question all answers are divided into three categories, namely *exemplary*, *acceptable* and *unacceptable*. For example, for the above question, answer (a) is exemplary, answer (b) is acceptable, and answer (c) is unacceptable.

In addition, for each question, a variant is defined with the *other* type of aggression (e.g., instrumental instead of emotional). For instance, such a variant for the above example would involve a passenger that is not emotional at all, but simply wants to use intimidation as an instrument to get a free ride. Also for these other variants, exemplary, acceptable and unacceptable answers are included in the database.[2] This allows the system to add extra difficulty by mixing up answers for both types of aggression. The types of answers that are included in the multiple-choice menu depend on the level the trainee is in, as explained in the next section.

4.3 Difficulty Levels

In order to make the dialog system adapt to the performance of the trainee, different levels of difficulty need to be distinguished. This way, the trainee can climb in levels when (s)he is performing well, and decline when many errors are made. For the proposed system, six levels of difficulty are used (see Table 1 for an overview):

1. Here, the type of aggression that is applicable to the current question (i.e., emotional or functional) is already revealed to the user, so all (s)he needs to do is to decide upon the appropriate response. Three potential answers are offered: one answer that is exemplary and two answers that are clearly wrong (the 'unacceptable' answers).
2. Similar to level 1, but the applicable type of aggression is not revealed anymore.
3. Similar to level 2, but instead of two 'unacceptable' answers, this time two 'acceptable' answers are provided, in addition to the 'exemplary' one. Hence, the main challenge for the user is to distinguish the exemplary answer from the acceptable ones.
4. Similar to level 3, but now the list of potential answers also includes an answer that is applicable to the type of aggression that is not applicable.
5. Similar to level 4, but now the difference between the answers is again more subtle (see Table 1), with makes it even harder to select the ideal one.
6. Similar to level 5, but with an additional time limit included. If no answer is selected before that time, the answer is considered unacceptable.

---

[2] Note that in some cases, answers that are unacceptable for one type of aggression may be exemplary for the other type. However, this is not necessarily always the case.

Table 1. Difficulty levels.

Level	Type of Aggression mentioned	Types of answers	Time limit
Level 1	Yes	2 × unacceptable for right type aggression	No
		1 × exemplary for right type aggression	
Level 2	No	2 × unacceptable for right type aggression	No
		1 × exemplary for right type aggression	
Level 3	No	2 × acceptable for right type aggression	No
		1 × exemplary for right type aggression	
Level 4	No	1 × acceptable or unacceptable for right type aggression	No
		1 × acceptable or unacceptable for wrong type of aggression	
		1 × exemplary for right type aggression	
Level 5	No	1 × acceptable or exemplary for wrong type aggression	No
		1 × acceptable for right type of aggression	
		1 × exemplary for right type aggression	
Level 6	No	1 × acceptable or exemplary for wrong type aggression	Yes
		1 × acceptable for right type of aggression	
		1 × exemplary for right type aggression	

In principle, the system determines at random whether it offers a case of emotional or instrumental aggression. However, if the trainee performs significantly worse on one type of aggression, that particular question type will be offered more often, to facilitate learning. Furthermore, also the order in which the answers are presented in the multiple-choice menu is determined randomly.

4.4   Transitions Between Levels

To determine when the difficulty level needs to increase or decrease, the system needs to keep track of the user's performance. This can be done by keeping score. Because the training will consist of different questions for the two types of aggression, for each type a separate score will be kept (as some trainees could be good in de-escalating one type of aggression, but may have difficulties with the other type). In order to reach a higher level, the score for both types of aggression needs to be sufficiently high to meet the demands of a level. To be a bit lenient, one error can be made without directly falling back a level.

The first part of the training (level 1–3) will focus on training the correct approach per aggression type. Once this is mastered, the second part of the training (level 4–6) will give answers that match reactions for both types of aggression, to test if the trainee can tell them apart. Levels are determined per aggression type separately, with one exception: after the first part of the training (i.e., level 1–3), the trainee needs to have

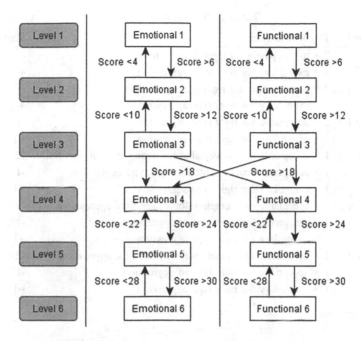

Fig. 2. Transitions between levels.

sufficient knowledge of both types of aggression before (s)he can continue. The transitions between levels are depicted in Fig. 2.

Scores below 0 in level 1 will remain zero. To complete the training, a score of 36 or higher is needed for both types of aggression.

Because each level has different combinations of answer types, the score for each type of answer is determined per level. The entire scoring mechanism is shown in Table 2 (note that this mechanism is the same for both types of aggression).

5   Implementation

In order to evaluate the conceptual model described above, it has been implemented using the Python programming language. For this implementation, abstract text-based questions have been used, as the intended VR was not yet fully functional. Nonetheless, this version implements the entire conceptual model and can be used within the VR environment with little effort.

To implement the model, a program has been written that loops through a number of different functions, as shown in Fig. 3. The double line shows where the loop starts at the beginning of the training, and where it stops at the end of the training. It will determine the level the trainee is in, and the *question type* that will be given (i.e., emotional or functional aggression). Given the level, it will determine the list of potential answers and present the question to the user. After the user gives input, the input is processed and the score is determined based on the given answer. If the trainee has got enough points for both types of aggression, the training ends.

Table 2. Scoring mechanism.

Level	Types of answers	Score
Level 1	2 × unacceptable for right type aggression	-1
	1 × exemplary for right type aggression	+1
Level 2	2 × unacceptable for right type aggression	-1
	1 × exemplary for right type aggression	+
Level 3	2 × acceptable for right type aggression	-1
	1 × exemplary for right type aggression	+1
Level 4	1 × acceptable or unacceptable for wrong type of aggression	-2
	1 × acceptable/unacceptable for right type aggression	-1
	1 × exemplary for right type aggression	+1
Level 5	1 × acceptable or exemplary for wrong type aggression	-2
	1 × acceptable for right type of aggression	-1
	1 × exemplary for right type aggression	+1
Level 6	1 × acceptable or exemplary for wrong type aggression	-2
	1 × acceptable for right type of aggression	-1
	1 × exemplary for right type aggression	+1

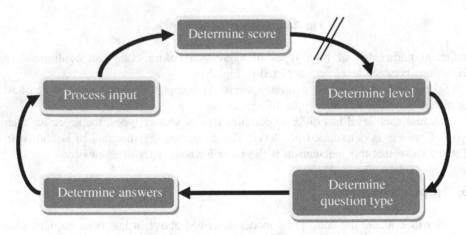

Fig. 3. The main functions of the implementation of the adaptive model.

Determine Level. Before a question can be selected, first the level the trainee is in has to be determined. Based on the current level and score, a decision is made whether or not to advance (or demote) the trainee to another level.

Start training. Part of this function is a sub-function which initializes the training for the current setup. This is only done the first time the trainee starts a training session.

Determine Question Type. As mentioned before, the type of aggression can be either emotional or functional. Normally, the type of question is selected at random. However, when the difference between the scores is larger than some predefined value d, questions will be selected for the type with the lowest score. Currently, a value of 5 is used for d.

Determine Answers. The options to appear in the multiple choice list presented to the trainee need to be carefully selected, depending on the current level of the trainee. Each conversation contains many possible responses to particular questions, categorized on aggression type and degree of correctness (unacceptable, acceptable, exemplary). Answers are selected for the current question according to the scheme depicted in Table 1. If there are more options for a particular answer, one is selected at random.

Process Input. At this point, all information about the current question to be presented to the user is available. For the interaction with the user, two sub-functions are created; the first presents the question to the user, while the second waits for his or her input.

Present Question. This function simply displays the current question, with the possible options displayed in the multiple choice list in random order. Only in the lowest level, the aggression type is shown to the user as well.

Process Input. The trainee can select his or her choice of answer by pressing the corresponding key on the keyboard. Only when the trainee is currently in the highest level, a time limit is imposed on the user. Otherwise, the trainee can take as much time as desired in coming to a decision on which response to give.

Determine Score. To determine the score, the given answer is evaluated based on the question type and correctness of the answer. Next, the score is updated based on the scheme presented in Table 2.

6 Preliminary Evaluation

To test whether the implementation works as described in the conceptual model, a number of functional evaluations have been performed. By systematically running the program for a number of test sessions, a range of information has been obtained about how the training progressed in different situations. Below, an overview is presented of the results of one illustrative test session, and an analysis is made of whether they correspond to the expected behavior.

First, in Figs. 4 and 5 below the scores are shown for functional and emotional aggression respectively. In gray on the background, the current level of the trainee for that type of aggression is displayed. Here, it can be seen that the score increases throughout the training and drops in some cases where incorrect answers are provided. Although it is difficult to see in these graphs, a closer inspection of the data has shown that this changing score follows the scheme as described in Table 2.

Focusing on level progression, Fig. 4 shows clearly that the levels increase if the trainee reaches the required score, except for level 4 which is only reached if the score for both types of aggression is sufficient. Looking at Fig. 5, the trainee's level decreases a couple of times after (s)he made a number of mistakes. However, when the trainee has reached level 4, and again makes some mistakes, the level does not drop back down to three, which is consistent with the intended behavior of the model.

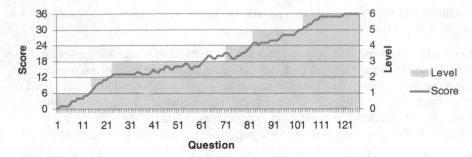

Fig. 4. Score for functional aggression over time with the corresponding level of the trainee.

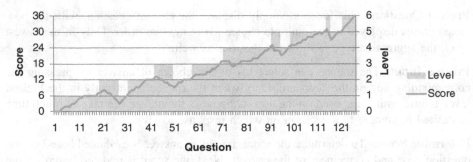

Fig. 5. Score for emotional aggression over time with the corresponding level of the trainee.

Another important aspect of this approach is the selection of the possible answers for each level. Figure 6 shows an overview of how the multiple choice options were distributed among the various categories of possible answers. As there are three options the trainee can choose from for each question, for each level always a third of the answers is from the category *exemplary*, meaning that there is always one exemplary option to choose from. In level 1 and 2, the other options come from the *unacceptable* category (with the difference between the levels being whether or not the type of aggression is given), while in level 3 *acceptable* answers are given as alternatives.

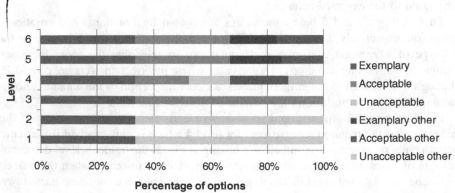

Fig. 6. Distribution of multiple choice options per level.

Starting from level 4, options for the other type of aggression are also given in such a manner that there is always one non-exemplary alternative for the right type of aggression and another alternative for the wrong type of aggression. In level 4, both alternatives can be of the unacceptable kind, while in level 5 it is either acceptable or en exemplary answer, but for the other type of aggression. Between level 5 and 6, no difference can be seen, as the only addition for level 6 is the time pressure.

To obtain these results, a few people have already worked with the adaptive system. Although this is not yet an extensive subjective evaluation, feedback from these users was of such a positive nature that we consider it noteworthy to mention here. Nevertheless, as discussed below, a more extensive evaluation of this adaptive training method is planned for the near future.

7 Discussion

Being able to de-escalate confrontations with aggressive individuals is a useful skill, in particular within professions where such confrontations are likely to happen, e.g., in the domains of public transport or public safety. Nevertheless, offering appropriate training that enables students to develop such skills is a nontrivial matter. In particular, existing (real world) training approaches are limited in terms of personalization: since the training is typically offered to groups of students together, it is hard to tune the content of training scenarios to individual needs.

As a complementary approach to real-world training, the current paper proposed a simulation-based environment for training of aggression de-escalation. The environment consists of a dialog system that allows a trainee to engage in a conversation with a (possibly aggressive) virtual agent. The agent can show aggressive behavior in terms of emotional speech, gestures and facial expressions. By observing these cues, the trainee needs to assess the situation (specifically: assess which type of aggression is shown) and select an appropriate response via a multiple choice menu.

The main focus of the current paper was on a module to make the system adaptive to the performance of the trainee. To this end, first a number of separate *learning goals* were identified, such as 'recognizing the type of aggression' and 'being able to make decisions under time pressure'. Based on these learning goals, a number of levels of difficulty were identified, as well as a mechanism to switch up and down between these levels based on the user's score. A preliminary evaluation demonstrated that the system successfully adapted its difficulty level to the performance of the user, and that users were generally positive about the effect of this adaptation mechanism.

Obviously, this finding should not be interpreted as a definitive proof that the adaptation mechanism results in quicker or better learning than a non-adaptive training system. To test this more specific hypothesis, future research will involve an experiment to systematically compare the effectiveness of the proposed training system with a non-adaptive one. Additionally, for follow-up research it will be interesting to compare the proposed (manual) adaptation mechanism with a mechanism in which the transitions between levels are learned automatically based on user performance data, and to explore possibilities of using data gathered across multiple trainees to improve the experience for any individual trainee.

Acknowledgments. This research was supported by funding from the National Initiative Brain and Cognition, coordinated by the Netherlands Organization for Scientific Research (NWO), under grant agreement No. 056-25-013.

References

1. Abraham, M., Flight, S., Roorda, W.: Agressie en geweld tegen werknemers met een publieke taak. Onderzoek voor Veilige Publieke Taak 2007 - 2009 - 2011. DSP, Amsterdam (2011). (in Dutch)
2. James, A., Madeley, R., Dove, A.: Violence and aggression in the emergency department. Emerg Med J. **23**(6), 431–434 (2006)
3. Rafaeli, A., Erez, A., Ravid, S., Derfler-Rozin, R., Treister, D.E., Scheyer, R.: When customers exhibit verbal aggression, employees pay cognitive costs. J. Appl. Psychol. **97**(5), 931–950 (2012)
4. Bonner, G., McLaughlin, S.: The psychological impact of aggression on nursing staff. Br J Nurs. **16**(13), 810–814 (2007)
5. Anderson, L.N., Clarke, J.T.: De-escalating verbal aggression in primary care settings. Nurse Pract, vol. 21(10), pp. 95, 98, 101–102 (1996)
6. Ministry of the Interior and Kingdom Relations. Handboek agressie en geweld - voorkomen, beperken, afhandelen. Technical report for the Programme 'Veilige Publieke Taak', April 2008. (in Dutch)
7. http://stress.few.vu.nl
8. Ritterfeld, U., Cody, M., Vorderer, P. (eds.): Serious Games: Mechanisms and Effects. Routledge, New York (2009)
9. Hulst, A. van der Muller, T., Besselink, S., Coetsier, D., Roos, C.: Bloody serious gaming: experiences with job oriented training. In: Proceedings of I/ITSEC 2008, pp. 375-385, Orlando, Fla, USA (2008)
10. Graafland, M., Schraagen, J.M., Schijven, M.P.: Systematic review of serious games for medical education and surgical skills training. Br. J. Surg. **99**(10), 1322–1330 (2012)
11. Kim, J., Hill, R.W., Durlach, P., Lane, H.C., Forbell, E., Core, C., Marsella, S., Pynadath, D., Hart, J.: BiLAT: a game-based environment for practicing negotiation in a cultural context. Int. J. AI Educ. **19**(3), 289–308 (2009)
12. Christoph, N.: The role of metacognitive skills in learning to solve problems. Ph.D. thesis. University of Amsterdam (2006)
13. Heuvelink, A., Mioch, T.: FeGA: a cognitive feedback generating agent. In: Proceedings of the Seventh IEEE/WIC/ACM International Conference on Intelligent Agent Technology (IAT 2008), pp. 567–572. IEEE Computer Society Press (2008)
14. Miller, J.D., Lyna, D.R.: Reactive and proactive aggression: similarities and differences. Personality Individ. Differ. **41**(8), 1469–1480 (2006)
15. Bandura, A.: Social learning and personality development. Holt, Rinehart, and Winston, New York (1963)
16. Berkowitz, L.: Whatever happened to the frustration-aggression hypothesis? American Behav. Sci. **21**, 691–708 (1978)
17. Angie, A.D., Connelly, S., Waples, E.P., Kligyte, V.: The influence of discrete emotions on judgment and decision-making: a meta-analytic review. Cogn. Emot. **25**(8), 1393–1422 (2011)

18. Hubbard, J.A., Smithmyer, C.M., Ramsden, S.R., Parker, E.H., Flanagan, K.D., Dearing, K. F., Relyea, N., Simons, R.F.: Observational, physiological, and self-report measures of children's anger: relations to reactive versus proactive aggression. Child Dev. **73**(4), 1101–1118 (2002)

19. Graham, S., Weiner, B.: Theories and principles of motivation. In: Berliner, D.C., Calfee, R. C. (eds.) Handbook of Educational Psychology, pp. 63–84. Simon & Schuster Macmillan, New York (1996)

20. Hoogen, W.M., van den IJsselsteijn, W.A., de Kort, Y.A.W., Poels, K:. Toward real-time behavioral indicators of player experiences: pressure patterns and postural responses. In: Proceedings of Measuring Behavior 2008, pp. 100–101 Maastricht, The Netherlands (2008)

21. Holmes, J., Gathercole, S.E., Dunning, D.L.: Adaptive training leads to sustained enhancement of poor working memory in children. Dev. Sci. **12**, F9–F15 (2009)

22. Wickens, C.D., Hutchins, S., Carolan, T.: Effectiveness of part-task training and increasing-difficulty training strategies, a meta-analysis approach. Hum. Factors **55**, 461–470 (2012)

23. Nogueira, P.A., Rodrigues, R., Oliveira, E., Nacke, L.E.: Guided emotional state regulation: understanding and shaping players' affective experiences in digital games. In: Proceedings of the Ninth AAAI Conference on Artificial Intelligence and Interactive Digital Entertainment, pp. 51–57 (2013)

24. Yannakakis, G.N., Togelius, J., Khaled, R., Jhala, A., Karpouzis, K., Paiva, A., Vasalou, A.: Siren: towards adaptive serious games for teaching conflict resolution. In: Meyer, B. (ed.) Proceedings of the 4th European Conference on Games Based Learning, pp.412–417 (2010)

25. Raybourn, E.M.: Applying simulation experience design methods to creating serious game-based adaptive training systems. Interacting with Computers **19**(2), 206–214 (2007). The American Digital Library 2007

26. Bosse, T., Gerritsen, C.: Scenario's GVB. VU University Amsterdam, Technical report (2014)

Robotic Simulation

Mobile GPGPU Acceleration of Embodied Robot Simulation

Simon Jones[1,2]([⊠]), Matthew Studley[1], and Alan Winfield[1]

[1] Bristol Robotics Laboratory, University of the West of England, Bristol, UK
[2] University of Bristol, Bristol, UK
simon.jones@brl.ac.uk, {matthew2.studley,alan.winfield}@uwe.ac.uk

Abstract. It is desirable for a robot to be able to run on-board simulations of itself in a model of the world to evaluate action consequences and test new controller solutions, but simulation is computationally expensive. Modern mobile System-on-Chip devices have high performance at low power consumption levels and now incorporate powerful graphics processing units, making them good potential candidates to host on-board simulations. We use the parallel language OpenCL on two such devices to accelerate the widely-used Stage robot simulator and demonstrate both higher simulation speed and lower energy use on a multi-robot benchmark. To the best of our knowledge, this is the first time that GPGPU on mobile devices have been used to accelerate robot simulation, and moves towards providing an autonomous robot with an embodied *what-if* capability.

1 Introduction

The capability of an autonomous robot to perform on-board simulations of reality is desirable for a number of reasons.

In the area of swarm robotics [20] the design of controllers to produce a desired emergent collective behaviour is notoriously hard. Some successful approaches use an evolutionary algorithm where controller solutions are evolved off-line in repeated simulations of a swarm of robots prior to implementation in real robots but the resultant controller is not adaptive to changing environmental conditions. It is possible to have communication links between robots and off-board simulations to give adapability but at the cost of autonomy. One approach to provide both adaptability and autonomy is to move the evolutionary algorithm and simulation onto the robots so that controllers can be evolved in response to the environment. O'Dowd et al. in [15,16] describe work in this area.

An on-board simulation might also be used to equip a robot with a 'functional imagination' [12] allowing a robot to evaluate courses of action or strategies in the safety of simulation, rather than in the real world where it may have potentially catastrophic consequences. Recent work by Winfield et al. [25] extends this to provide a robot with a form of 'ethical' action selection, where a robot has an internal model which it can use to make predictions about the consequences of both its own and others actions through simulation of multiple scenarios and even act to

© Springer International Publishing Switzerland 2015
C.J. Headland et al. (Eds.): ALIA 2014, CCIS 519, pp. 97–109, 2015.
DOI: 10.1007/978-3-319-18084-7_8

prevent danger to another robot. Currently this capability is dependent on a wifi link to a laptop due to the lack of sufficient on-board processing power. Clearly, where this *what-if* capability is safety critical or inherent in the behaviour of the robot, as in the 'ethical' robot above, it would not be possible to use an unreliable communications link and embodied simulation would be essential.

In both cases, the performance of the on-board simulation is critical in two ways. Firstly, simulation speed. Faster simulations allow larger numbers of robots, more scenarios, and longer simulated times within a given real time. Secondly, energy usage. Energy is a precious resource in a mobile robot and minimising the energy cost of performing a given simulation is an important goal.

Over the last decade, the performance of desktop PC graphics processors (GPU) in GFLOPS has outstripped that of CPUs and the emergence of parallel programming APIs such as CUDA [14], and more recently OpenCL [8], have made General Purpose Programming on the Graphics Processor (GPGPU) more accessible. GPGPU techniques are now widely used in scientific computing. This trend on the desktop is being mirrored on mobile platforms but within a far more restrictive power envelope; current mobile devices are as powerful as the desktop of around ten years ago but with power consumption at least an order of magnitude lower.[1]

Performing computation on a GPU is generally more energy efficient at a given performance level than performing the same computation on a CPU, provided the problem can be expressed in a suitably parallel way, because the CPU has to devote large amounts of silicon area to structures designed to extract instruction level parallelism while preserving the illusion of the semantically serial instruction stream, and will also generally run at a higher clock frequency. The GPU, on the other hand, is explicitly parallel and a much larger proportion of the silicon area can be devoted to performing computation rather than control. The design goal is massively multi-threaded throughput rather than single thread performance. See Keckler et al. [7] for a good discussion of these trends.

Stage is a widely used 2D robot sensorimotor simulator that is capable of simulating large populations of robots. Vaughan [21] introduces version 3 of Stage and examines its performance scalability, demonstrating near-linear execution time scaling with populations up to 100000 robots when each robot is running an identical simple controller. Vaughan also proposes a method of benchmarking the performance.

It is clear that accelerating Stage using GPGPU techniques could have wide applicability, both on and off robotic platforms. In this paper we present a method to apply OpenCL acceleration to the central time-consuming functionality of Stage without requiring a major re-write. We then evaluate its performance on the Samsung Exynos 5250 and 5420 SoCs, both mobile GPGPU capable devices, demonstrating a speed increase of 82 % and a drop in energy usage of 30 % for some benchmarks, compared to the unaccelerated software on the same platform.

---

[1] Nvidia 6800 Ultra 40 GFLOPS, 100 W, Pentium 4 7 GFLOPS [11]. Chromebook with Samsung Exynos 5250 72 GFLOPS GPU, 27 GFLOPS CPU, <7 W.

2   Previous Work

The scalability of Stage is measured and discussed in Vaughan [21], along with a good overview and some discussion of the internal structure and design choices. Piniciroli et al. [19] describe a different robot simulator and also measure its performance using a similar methodology to that described by Vaughan.

An early demonstration of the use of evolutionary algorithms to design swarm robot controllers is given by Dorigo et al. in [3] where controllers for two different collective tasks are evolved within a simplified simulation which are then tested within a high fidelity physics-based simulation. Hauert et al. [5] tackle the problem of adaptability of evolved controllers by reverse engineering and parameterising them. O'Dowd et el in [15,16] move towards providing robustness to environmental change by using a distributed evolutionary algorithm on board a swarm of e-puck [13] robots, with simple reality simulations running on the Linux Extension Board [9]. This allows the co-evolution both of the simulated environment and the swarm controllers.

Bongard et al. in [1] use a process of continuous self modelling to give a robot the ability to autonomously detect and compensate for damage. Vaughan and Zuluaga [22] introduce the use of self simulation to provide a form of imagination, whereby a robot can safely evaluate different courses of action in simulation before applying them in the real world. This is taken further by Winfield et al. in [25] who describe using simulation to give a robot the ability to predict the consequence of both its own and others actions and then using this to provide an 'ethical' action selection mechanism.

Ohkura et al. [17] demonstrate performance benefits from using CUDA on a desktop GPU to accelerate the evolution of a swarm robotics controller for a food-foraging problem. Wang et al. [23,24] and Kang et al. [6] both demonstrate performance benefits through the use of OpenCL on mobile devices to accelerate image processing algorithms. Maghazeh et al. [10] investigate the performance and energy efficiency of five different non-graphic benchmarks implemented in OpenCL on a mobile device, showing benefits with most but noting the need to consider different optimisation strategies compared to desktop GPUs. Grasso et al. [4] evaluate the ARM Mali GPU of the Exynos 5250 SoC for energy efficient HPC usage, porting a number of benchmarks to OpenCL and demonstrating average speedups of 8.7x and energy consumption of only 32 % compared to an ARM A15 CPU core.

3   Accelerating Stage

We briefly discuss the internals of Stage, particularly the ray tracing operation that is the most time consuming operation and outline how we used OpenCL to accelerate this functionality. Our goal was to make as few changes to the code of Stage as possible because we wished to minimise both development risk and time, and demonstrate a proof-of-concept rather than an optimised solution[2].

---

[2] The modified source code is available at https://bitbucket.org/siteks/stage_opencl.

3.1 Overview of Stage Internals

Stage is a mature, well optimised piece of software, written in C++. All entities within the simulated world are based on the *Model* class and its derivatives, which include things like *ModelPosition* two-wheeled motion kinematics and *ModelRanger* range sensors. Each instance of *Model* can have physical characteristics such as geometry within the world, represented as *blocks*, which are polygons in the XY plane with Z extents ('two and a half D'). The space of the world is a discrete grid, and the presence of geometry within the world grid is represented internally with a sparse data structure.

The *ModelRanger* derivative class implements range sensing and is used to model sensors such as laser range finders and ultrasonic sensors. The process of modelling range sensing is implemented by performing a ray tracing operation using Cohen's algorithm [2] through the sparse occupancy grid from the location of the sensor. At every grid location, each block at that location is checked to see if it has Z extents that cover the Z position of the sensor, and then a predicate function is invoked on the block to ensure it both doesn't belong to the model the sensor belongs to, and is visible to the sensor. Other *Model* derivative classes such as *ModelBlobfinder* define this predicate function differently.

This ray tracing operation is the most time consuming part of the simulation, typically taking upwards of 90 % of the execution time.

The sparse data structure representing the world grid divides the space into 32×32 squares of cells called *regions*, and 32×32 squares of regions called *superregions*. Only regions and superregions which actually contain geometry are represented, which saves memory and allows the ray tracing function to skip over known empty parts of the world.

Every simulation timestep, the following simplified sequence takes place: Firstly, all the *ModelPosition* models have their geometry moved within the world grid, being removed from old locations and redrawn into their new locations. Then all the *ModelRanger* models perform ray tracing through the world grid to create sensor data. Finally, all the robot controllers are updated. This sequence repeats until the end of the simulation.

3.2 OpenCL Acceleration Strategy

As illustrated in Fig. 1, the process of ray tracing involves checking every location within the world grid along the path of a ray from the sensor to the limit of the sensor range or until there is an intersection with an object. The sparse nature of the data structure means that known empty regions of the world can be skipped over, but checking for the presence of geometry dominates execution time.

Each ray is completely independent, except for traversing the same world data structure, making ray tracing a parallel problem well suited to running on a GPU. The problem with using OpenCL to accelerate ray tracing in Stage is the use of an arbitrary predicate function for testing whether an occupied grid cell on the ray path is actually an intersection. An OpenCL kernel exists in a different memory space and has no knowledge of the data structures of the host,

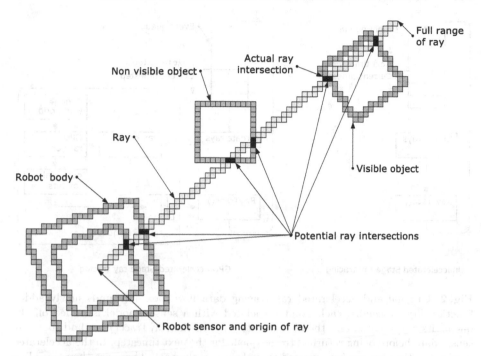

Fig. 1. Ray tracing process. In order to model a sensor, each cell of the world grid along the path of the ray is visited in turn to check if there is anything at that location. There may be many potential ray intersections before an actual intersection that corresponds to the sensor detecting an object. Objects within the world are shown as dark grey, the path of the ray as light grey, and potential intersections as black cells. The first four intersections are with the robots own geometry, which is not regarded as a hit, then there are four more with a non-visible object, perhaps because its Z position is below that of the sensor. Finally there is an actual intersection, at this point the ray trace function would normally terminate.

and no way to easily interpret them even if they were made available[3]. Making the intersection test a fixed function would radically and unacceptably change the behaviour and flexibility of Stage, keeping the functionality while performing all ray tracing on the GPU would require a major rewrite.

The solution we chose was to perform the parallel ray tracing on the GPU using a minimal version of the world grid data structure, and create a list of *potential* intersections for each ray. This information is then be used by the normal Stage ray trace function to skip over all cells now known not to contain any geometry and only apply the predicate test to occupied cells. Complete functionality is preserved.

This is illustrated in Fig. 2. At each timestep, two data structures representing all the rays and a minimal world occupancy grid are prepared and made available to the GPU. The OpenCL kernel version of the ray trace algorithm is invoked on

---

[3] The data structures are composed of C++ classes, while OpenCL is based on C99.

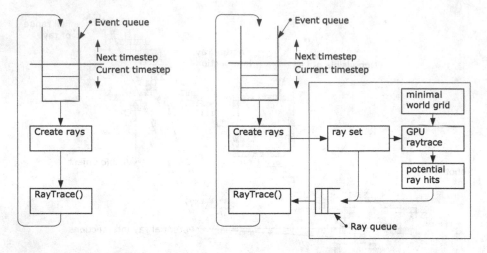

Unaccelerated Stage ray tracing   GPU accelerated Stage ray tracing

Fig. 2. Original and accelerated ray tracing data flow, box surrounds newly added functionality. Normally, each event associated with a sensor model is pulled off the queue, its rays created and then immediately fed to the RayTrace() method to create sensor data before being returned to the queue for the next timestep. In the accelerated version, all the rays are first created to make a complete set. These are then traced on the GPU using a minimal representation of the world occupancy grid to generate a set of potential ray intersections. The created rays are then fed to the RayTrace() method in the expected order but with the additional information allowing empty cells to be skipped.

this data and runs in parallel across all the rays to the extent that the hardware allows, generating the potential ray hits data structure. This, and the rays, are fed back to the RayTrace() method, enhanced to allow it to skip over the cells now known to be empty.

There is obviously a certain amount of additional processing overhead that didn't exist before; preparing the world grid and ray set, making buffers available to the GPU, and bringing the potential intersection data back again. In a desktop GPU, the overhead is exacerbated by the need to copy data to the distinct memory of the GPU, but mobile SoCs typically have a unified memory architecture. In addition, each individual ray tracing thread of execution on the GPU will be much slower than on the CPU, we gain only when there are enough rays to trace in parallel. What might that number be? The ARM Mali T604 GPU has four cores, each with 256 threads, so we expect that we will need thousands of rays to show performance gains.

4   Testing Methodology

In order to evaluate the effectiveness of the acceleration of Stage, we propose two figures of merit and a series of benchmark scenarios. We then run the benchmarks on the target systems, measuring the power consumption and run times for both normal and accelerated versions of Stage.

4.1 Figures of Merit

Since we are interested in both the speed and the energy cost of simulation, as well as the scalability of the our acceleration with numbers of robots, we use two figures of merit. The first, r_{ACC}, is a measure of how much faster than real time an individual robot is simulated, defined as:

$$r_{ACC} = \frac{n \cdot t_{SIM}}{t_{MEAS}} \tag{1}$$

where n is the number of robots, t_{SIM} is the simulated time, and t_{MEAS} is the measured run time. The second, r_{EPSS}, is a measure of how much energy is consumed to simulate each robot for one simulated second. This is defined as:

$$r_{EPSS} = \frac{P_{RUN} \cdot t_{MEAS}}{n \cdot t_{SIM}} = \frac{P_{RUN}}{r_{ACC}} \tag{2}$$

where P_{RUN} is the average power consumption of the system while running the benchmark.

Some previous work on mobile GPGPU, Maghazeh et al. [10], uses the difference between idle and running power when making energy cost measurements, while other work, Pathania et al. [18], considers the total system energy cost. We take the latter approach since it is more conservative, taking the view that the entire system is necessary in order to run the benchmark. A system designer may be able to reduce this overhead but never eliminate it. An on-board simulation can only be of use to a robot if there is enough power to run the robot too.

4.2 Benchmarks

We use a similar methodology to that described by Vaughan [21], using two worlds, *cave*, and *hospital*, populated with an increasing number of robots, each running an identical maximum dispersal controller. As Vaughan points out, this represents a worst-case scenario for a ray-tracing simulator like Stage, since it maximises the space through which rays must propagate. The characteristics of the two benchmark series are summarised in Table 1.

The *cave* series uses the simple Pioneer 2DX robot model supplied with stage, which has a laser scanner range finder with 180 samples, and 16 ultrasonic range finders, each with a single sample. The robot body geometry is modelled with two polygons. The maximum number of robots simulated is 1000.

The *hospital* series uses a much larger world based on the hospital section bitmap supplied with Stage, with a smaller simpler robot. The body is only a single polygon with fewer sides, and just a laser sensor, though extended to a 350 degree field of view with a sample per degree. The maximum number of robots with *hospital* is 10000.

In both series, we measure the real time taken to simulate 600 s of simulated time, and the total energy consumed, for each of the population numbers. In all cases, the tests are run with graphics disabled.

Table 1. Benchmarks

	cave	hospital
Size	64 m × 64 m	540 m × 220 m
Resolution	0.02 m	0.1 m
Grid locations	1×10^7	1.2×10^7
Robots	1-1000	1-10000
Robot size	0.4 m × 0.4 m	0.24 m × 0.24 m
Sensors per robot	16 sonar + 180 sample laser	350 sample laser
Rays per robot	196	350

4.3   Target Devices

We targeted two mobile devices; the Samsung Chromebook and the Arndale
Octa development board. We used these devices because they both have a
System-on-Chip (SoC) with a GPU that supports the OpenCL language. The
Samsung Chromebook is a low-cost lightweight laptop that runs the Chrome
browser-based operating system. It is based on a Samsung Exynos 5250 SoC.
The Arndale Octa is based around a more recent Samsung Exynos 5420 SoC.
Some relevant specifications are shown in Table 2.

Table 2. Technical specifications of the two systems used. Note that due to limitations
in the available Linux kernel it was only possible to run the Octa CPU at 800 MHz. System power values are typical, measured with the screen turned off for the Chromebook
and with an accelerated Stage simulation running for the busy power.

	Samsung Chromebook	Arndale Octa
System-on-chip	Samsung Exynos 5250	Samsung Exynos 5420
CPU	Dual A15	Quad A15 + Quad A7
Max CPU frequency	1.7 GHz	1.8 GHz
Max CPU GFLOPS	27	58
GPU	ARM Mali T604	ARM Mali T628 MP6
Max GPU frequency	533 MHz	600 MHz
Max GPU GFLOPS	72	122
System idle power	1.8 W	1.2 W
System busy power	3.5 W	2.7 W

4.4   Energy Measurement

We measured the power by using 50 mR current sensing resistor in series with
the system power supply, and measuring both the voltage drop across it and

the voltage of the supply. The voltages were sampled at 10 ms intervals while a simulation was running and the product integrated to give a value for the total energy used for the simulation.

5   Results

Performance of unaccelerated Stage across the range of robot populations on all platforms and benchmarks showed the expected linear execution time. Energy usage was also relatively flat across the range. The GPU accelerated Stage performs poorly at low robot numbers, particularly for energy use, which is expected, but then overtakes the CPU-only version at higher robot population numbers. Figure 3 shows the results for the *hospital* series running on the Arndale Octa board. The other three results are omitted for brevity but show the same general picture, see Fig. 4 for a comparison.

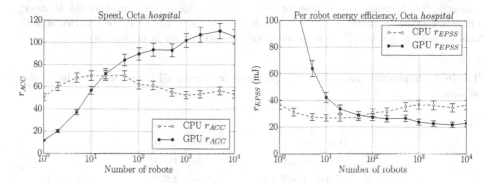

Fig. 3. Arndale Octa *hospital*. The CPU performance is broadly flat across the whole range of robot populations, demonstrating roughly linear scaling as described by Vaughan [21]. GPU performance is poor at low robot populations but exceeds the CPU in both speed and energy efficiency once above a population of 100 robots, or 35000 rays.

Figure 4 shows the relative performance between the GPU and CPU versions across all combinations of benchmark and hardware platform demonstrating the expected characteristics of a massively parallel throughput engine in that performance gains are not apparent until the level of parallelisation is high. Table 3 shows the points where the GPU performance reaches that of the CPU. The Arndale Octa and Chromebook show almost identical behaviour with regard to energy efficiency, but the break-even points for speed are much higher with the Chromebook than the Octa, probably due to the higher relative performance of the GPU compared to the CPU on the Octa.

We summarise the performance gains from GPU acceleration in Fig. 5. Taking the average for all data points with a population of 100 robots or more, there are clear benefits across all benchmark and hardware combinations with both figures of merit.

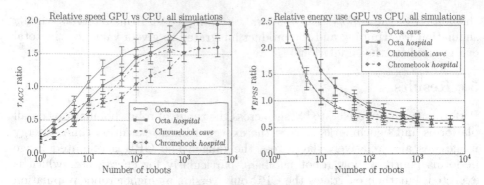

Fig. 4. The relative performance between the GPU accelerated and the CPU versions of Stage shows broad similarities across all four combinations of simulation series and hardware targets. Somewhere between a population of 10 to 100 robots, performance in both speed and energy efficiency on the GPU exceeds that of the unaccelerated software. The Chromebook demonstrates lower speed gains but almost identical energy efficiency gains with the GPU. The best improvement is the Octa *cave* series at 2000 robots, with at least 82 % increase in speed and 30 % drop in energy use.

Table 3. Break-even points for GPU performance versus CPU performance in number of rays.

	r_{ACC}	r_{EPSS}
Octa *cave*	1800	2200
Octa *hospital*	7000	21000
Chromebook *cave*	7800	2200
Chromebook *hospital*	32000	18000

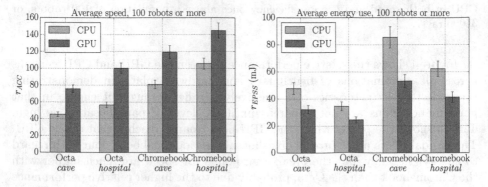

Fig. 5. Average performance at 100 robots or more.

6   Conclusions and Further Work

We have demonstrated a proof-of-concept GPU acceleration of the robot simulator Stage showing both simulation speed and energy efficiency gains. There are many further avenues down which this work can be taken.

In this initial proof-of-concept, we focussed on maximising benefit for minimal development risk. We intend to investigate many further optimisations of this approach. The execution on GPU and CPU can be overlapped, the construction of the data structures for the GPU could be made much faster, and a smart allocation of rays to GPU cores could increase speed by improving cache behaviour through increasing locality of access within the world grid data structure. In addition, alternative ray tracing algorithms may be a better fit for the characteristics of a GPU.

We intend to adapt our approach to support further work on the 'consequence engine' described in Winfield et al. [25] in which each of the simulation scenarios contain only a few robots. By constructing a world containing many such scenarios arranged in a grid, we can have a single simulation with many robots, such that GPU acceleration will be beneficial. An essential requirement for such an 'ethical' robot is that *what-if* simulations are conducted embodied in the robot, rather than at the other end of an unreliable communications link. Accelerated simulation on a low-power mobile platform moves towards that goal, and we also intend to equip e-puck robots with mobile GPU hardware to demonstrate embodied simulation.

The use of mobile System-on-Chip devices with GPUs opens new possibilities for robot self simulation. This paper demonstrates the viability of one possible approach and points the way towards autonomous robots with *what-if* capability.

References

1. Bongard, J., Zykov, V., Lipson, H.: Resilient machines through continuous self-modeling. Science **314**(5802), 1118–1121 (2006)
2. Cohen-Or, D., Kaufman, A.: 3D line voxelization and connectivity control. IEEE Comput. Graphics Appl. **17**(6), 80–87 (1997)
3. Dorigo, M., Trianni, V., Şahin, E., Groß, R., Labella, T.H., Baldassarre, G., Nolfi, S., Deneubourg, J.-L., Mondada, F., Floreano, D., et al.: Evolving self-organizing behaviors for a swarm-bot. Auton. Robots **17**(2–3), 223–245 (2004)
4. Grasso, I., Radojkovic, P., Rajovic, N., Gelado, I., Ramirez, A.: Energy efficient hpc on embedded socs: optimization techniques for mali GPU. In: 2014 IEEE 28th International Parallel and Distributed Processing Symposium, pp. 123–132. IEEE (2014)
5. Hauert, S., Zufferey, J.-C., Floreano, D.: Reverse-engineering of artificially evolved controllers for swarms of robots. In: IEEE Congress on Evolutionary Computation, CEC 2009, pp. 55–61. IEEE (2009)
6. Kang, S.H., Lee, S-J., Park, I.K.: Parallelization and optimization of feature detection algorithms on embedded gpu. In: International Workshop on Advanced Image Technology (2014)

7. Keckler, S.W., Dally, W.J., Khailany, B., Garland, M., Glasco, D.: Gpus and the future of parallel computing. IEEE Micro **31**(5), 7–17 (2011)
8. Khronos OpenCL Working Group et al: The OpenCL Specification, Version 1.1 (2010)
9. Liu, W., Winfield, A.F.T.: Open-hardware e-puck linux extension board for experimental swarm robotics research. Microprocess. Microsyst. **35**(1), 60–67 (2011)
10. Maghazeh, A., Bordoloi, U.D., Eles, P., Peng, Z.: General purpose computing on low-power embedded gpus: has it come of age? In: 2013 International Conference on Embedded Computer Systems: Architectures, Modeling, and Simulation (SAMOS XIII), pp. 1–10. IEEE (2013)
11. Manocha, D.: General-purpose computations using graphics processors. Computer **38**(8), 85–88 (2005)
12. Marques, H.G., Holland, O.: Architectures for functional imagination. Neurocomputing **72**(4), 743–759 (2009)
13. Mondada, F., Bonani, M., Raemy, X., Pugh, J., Cianci, C., Klaptocz, A., Magnenat, S., Zufferey, J-C., Floreano, D., Martinoli, A.: The e-puck, a robot designed for education in engineering. In: Proceedings of the 9th conference on autonomous robot systems and competitions, vol. 1, pp. 59–65 (2009)
14. Nvidia: NVIDIA CUDA, Compute Unified Device Architecture Programming Guide. NVIDIA, Santa Clara, CA, USA (2007)
15. O'Dowd, P., Winfield, A.F.T., Studley, M.: Towards accelerated distributed evolution for adaptive behaviours in swarm robotics. In: Belpaeme, T., Bugmann, G., Melhuish, C., Witkowski, M. (eds.) Towards Autonomous Robotic Systems. pp. 169–175. University of Plymouth (2010)
16. O'Dowd, P.J., Winfield, A.F.T., Studley, M.: The distributed co-evolution of an embodied simulator and controller for swarm robot behaviours. In: 2011 IEEE/RSJ International Conference on Intelligent Robots and Systems (IROS), pp. 4995–5000. IEEE (2011)
17. Ohkura, K., Yasuda, T., Matsumura, Y., Kadota, M.: GPU implementation of food-foraging problem for evolutionary swarm robotics systems. In: Dorigo, M., Birattari, M., Garnier, S., Hamann, H., Montes de Oca, M., Solnon, C., Stützle, T. (eds.) ANTS 2014. LNCS, vol. 8667, pp. 238–245. Springer, Heidelberg (2014)
18. Pathania, A., Jiao, Q., Prakash, A., Mitra, T.: Integrated cpu-gpu power management for 3D mobile games. In: Proceedings of the The 51st Annual Design Automation Conference on Design Automation Conference, DAC 2014, pp. 40:1–40:6. ACM, New York (2014)
19. Pinciroli, C., Trianni, V., O'Grady, R., Pini, G., Brutschy, A., Brambilla, M., Mathews, N., Ferrante, E., Caro, G.D., Ducatelle, F. et al: Argos: a modular, multi-engine simulator for heterogeneous swarm robotics. In: 2011 IEEE/RSJ International Conference on Intelligent Robots and Systems (IROS), pp. 5027–5034. IEEE (2011)
20. Şahin, E.: Swarm robotics: from sources of inspiration to domains of application. In: Şahin, E., Spears, W.M. (eds.) Swarm Robotics 2004. LNCS, vol. 3342, pp. 10–20. Springer, Heidelberg (2005)
21. Vaughan, R.: Massively multi-robot simulation in stage. Swarm Intell. **2**(2–4), 189–208 (2008)
22. Vaughan, R.T., Zuluaga, M.: Use your illusion: sensorimotor self-simulation allows complex agents to plan with incomplete self-knowledge. In: Nolfi, S., Baldassarre, G., Calabretta, R., Hallam, J.C.T., Marocco, D., Meyer, J.-A., Miglino, O., Parisi, D. (eds.) SAB 2006. LNCS (LNAI), vol. 4095, pp. 298–309. Springer, Heidelberg (2006)

23. Wang, G., Xiong, Y., Yun, J., Cavallaro, J.R.: Accelerating computer vision algorithms using opencl framework on the mobile gpu-a case study. In: 2013 IEEE International Conference on Acoustics, Speech and Signal Processing (ICASSP), pp. 2629–2633. IEEE (2013)

24. Wang, G., Xiong, Y., Yun, J., Cavallaro, J.R.: Computer vision accelerators for mobile systems based on opencl gpgpu co-processing. J. Sig. Process. Syst. **76**(3), 283–299 (2014)

25. Winfield, A.F.T., Blum, C., Liu, W.: Towards an ethical robot: internal models, consequences and ethical action selection. In: Mistry, M., Leonardis, A., Witkowski, M., Melhuish, C. (eds.) TAROS 2014. LNCS, vol. 8717, pp. 85–96. Springer, Heidelberg (2014)

Ashby's Mobile Homeostat

Steve Battle[✉]

Sysemia Ltd., Bristol and Bath Science Park, Dirac Crescent,
Emerson's Green, Bristol BS16 7FR, UK
steve.battle@sysemia.co.uk
http://www.stevebattle.me

Abstract. In *Design for a Brain*, W. Ross Ashby speculates about the possibility of creating a mobile homeostat "with its critical states set so that it seeks situations of high illumination." This paper explores a realization of Ashby's homeostat within a simulated robot and environment exploring the question as to whether the classic homeostat architecture is able to adapt to this environment. Remaining faithful to the physical design of Ashby's device, this simulation enables us to quantitatively evaluate Ashby's proposition that homeostasis can be achieved through *ultrastability*. Following his *law of requisite variety* it is demonstrated that increasing the number of units increases the time taken to reach equilibrium, and that conversely, reducing internal connectivity reduces the time taken to reach equilibrium.

Keywords: Homeostat · Ultrastability · Robotics · Ashby

1 Introduction

Attendees of the ninth Macy Conference on Cybernetics in 1952 were presented with an account of an astonishing machine called the homeostat [9]. Completed in March 1948, its inventor was W. Ross Ashby, Research Director at Barnwood House Hospital in Gloucester. The homeostat comprised four functional units constructed from ex-RAF bomb control switch-gear kits, identified by the colours red, green, blue, and yellow[1]. Each unit represents a single variable, each one acting on all the other units resulting in a complex pattern of behaviour. As a physical model it allowed Ashby to demonstrate his principle of *ultrastability* and the *law of requisite variety*. The homeostat's most challenging feature, which many found counter-intuitive, was its bias towards inaction. It was no wonder then that Cyberneticist Julian Bigelow famously asked, "whether this particular model has any relation to the nervous system? It may be a beautiful replica of something, but heaven only knows what."[9].

Completed in March 1948[2], the most distinctive features of the 'Automatic homeostat' are the indicator needles that sit atop each unit and provide the

---

[1] W. Ross Ashby journals, vol.12, p2747, February 1950.
[2] W. Ross Ashby journals, vol.11, p2435, 16th March 1948.

© Springer International Publishing Switzerland 2015
C.J. Headleand et al. (Eds.): ALIA 2014, CCIS 519, pp. 110–123, 2015.
DOI: 10.1007/978-3-319-18084-7_9

read-out for each variable. Each unit takes input from every other unit, and their effect on the needle is determined by a combination of a potentiometer and commutator that change the magnitude and polarity of the input voltage. A group of magnetic coils sum these weighted inputs to deflect the needle from its central position, "The position of the needle provides a beautiful functionator to get a linear function of the inputs."[3] However, these needles not only provide a read-out of the state the homeostat, but are integral to its function. They pick up a small electrical potential from a vane that dips into a trough of water. This signal is amplified and adjusted via a resistive load so that the output is proportional to the needle's deviation from the central position. When the needle is central the output is zero. The movement of the vanes through the water also provides a useful dampening effect, slowing the system dynamics to a human timescale.

The input weights can be changed using an electro-mechanical uniselector which allows a random selection from 25 resistances and polarities. This selector not only affords plasticity in weighting but also in connectivity, "Zeros occur, and when this happens the units are, in effect, cut off from one another" [9]. One of the inputs to the unit is a feedback loop from its own output which is not under uniselector control but may be set manually. This provides first-order positive or negative feedback creating oscillations that are a source of the dynamic behaviour of the homeostat. All the experiments presented in this paper are conducted with negative feedback.

The linear equations of the homeostat are defined in the appendices of *Design for a Brain* [2] and are represented in Eq. 1 below, assuming four units as in the original homeostat ($1 \leq i \leq 4$).

$$\frac{dx_i}{dt} = \dot{x}_i$$
$$\frac{d\dot{x}_i}{dt} = h \sum_{k=1}^{4} a_{i,k} x_k - j\dot{x}_i \tag{1}$$

The variables x_i represent the outputs of the four homeostat units. The signed weights $a_{i,k}$ combine the potentiometer and commutator settings. The factor h controls the torque acting on the read-out needle through an induction coil, and j is the ratio of the viscosity of the fluid in the trough to the moment of inertia of the magnet, determining the rate of change.

A contemporary of Ross Ashby (and fellow member of the Ratio club [14]), W. Grey Walter inventor of the first autonomous robots, likened the homeostat to a "fireside cat or dog which only stirs when disturbed, and then methodically finds a comfortable position and goes to sleep again" leading him to describe the homeostat as *Machina sopora* [16]. Walter was contrasting the behaviour of the homeostat with his own Machina speculatrix which exhibited a more lively, exploratory behavior, "a typical animal propensity is to explore the environment rather than to wait passively for something to happen." Yet the explorations of

---

[3] W. Ross Ashby journals, vol.9, p2095, December 1946.

M. speculatrix would be all for nought in the face of a fundamental change in the environment threatening the very survival of the robot. An organism cannot simply ignore such extreme conditions but must act to remedy the causes of the problem. Franchi [10] traces these ideas back to Sigmund Freud's' Project for a Scientific Psychology' [12], "The organism cannot withdraw itself from [the major needs] as it does from external stimuli." In a fickle environment the homeostat comes into its own.

Ashby's great innovation was the double feedback loop, augmenting the conventional sensorimotor loop. This models how an organism detects conditions that threaten its survival and its escape strategy which "changed one machine into another." [4] A subset of homeostat units are deemed *essential* variables with lower and upper acceptable limits. When the limits on an essential variable are exceeded the output current for that unit is sufficient to close a relay. When this occurs in conjunction with a system clock it triggers the unit's uniselector reconfiguring the unit at random. After some time the homeostat hits upon a configuration that achieves equilibrium in its new environment. This is adaptation through *ultrastability*.

The mathematical model presented in Eq. 1 above, assume a linear relationship between the inputs and the visible output. In the physical realization of the homeostat it is (approximately) linear only in the range $\pm 45°$ either side of the needle centre. As Ashby notes, the system may be "unstable and self-aggravating, running away to the limits of the troughs." When the needle hits one of the end-stops of the trough, the needle can move no further and thus the output *saturates* at that value. This is a classic saturating linear function. The full simulation models this effect with the outputs saturating at the points of low and high potential.

An experiment from Ashby's *Design for a Brain*[4] is reproduced here. He was impressed by the ability of the nervous system to adapt to surgical reversals of muscles and nerve fibres. This experiment demonstrates an analogous effect in the homeostat by reversing the polarity of the connection between two units. This is illustrated in Fig. 1 where unit 1 (solid line) represents the trace of an essential variable with bounds $[-1, 1]$, while unit 2 (dashed line) is under manual control.

In this scenario the needles were used as input devices by Ashby physically deflecting a needle one way or the other. The output of unit 1 indicated by the solid line shows how the system adapts to the manual deflections of unit 2. This is modelled in the simulation by the addition of a given (simulated) voltage. A baseline deflection of 0.2 volts is added to unit 2 throughout the experiment except at the deflection points D1 & D2 when this is raised to 0.3 volts. After an initial settling time (from $t = 0$) the units adjust to the baseline deflection. At point D1 ($t = 50$) the deflection of unit 2 is briefly raised to 0.3 volts and unit 1 can be seen to follow in the same direction.

Following D1 the deflection is returned to the baseline. Without this baseline the magnitude at R1 would be zero and the reversal of polarity would have

---

[4] Design for a Brain, 2nd edition, Sect. 8/4.

no effect. At point R1 ($t = 100$) the polarity of the connection from unit 1 to
unit 2 is reversed under manual control. This in turn causes instability in unit
1 that transgresses the limits of the essential variable, causing a step-change in
the weights connecting unit 2 back to unit 1. Now, when the same deflection
is applied at D2 ($t = 150$) the response of unit 1 is to move in the opposite
direction. The manual reversal in unit 2 at R1 is balanced by an automatic
weight reversal in the selector of unit 1.

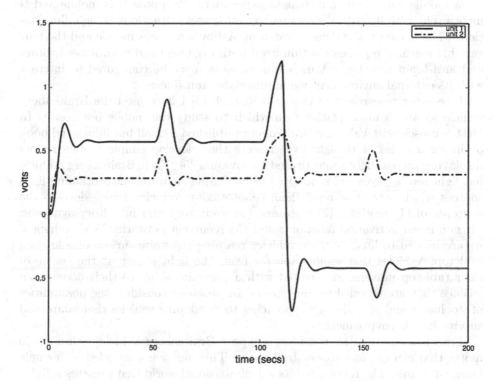

Fig. 1. Two units interacting. Identical deflections applied at D1 and D2 to unit 2
(dashed line) have opposite effects on unit 1 (solid line) after polarity reversal at R1
and subsequent recovery of stability.

A MATLAB simulation reproducing this scenario is included in Appendix A.
The parameters are set as follows: $h = 1.0$, $j = 1.0$ with negative feedback on
each unit of -0.5. The weight from unit 1 to unit 2 is initially -0.1, reversed
at R1. The weight from unit 2 to unit 1 changes from 1.0 to -0.668, a value
drawn from observation of the full homeostat simulation and known to result
in a stable solution. The behaviour of the uniselector is not included in this
version of the simulation. Like other simulations [8,13] the aim is to capture
the key features of Ashby's homeostat including the linear equations of Eq. 1,
essential bounds on variables and environmental coupling consistent with the
architecture of the homeostat. The full simulation is based on Euler's forward

method which provides a rapid iterative approach that lends itself to solving differential equations in real-time. For all the experiments in this paper the essential variables are bounded to the range $[-1, 1]$.

2   The Mobile Homeostat

In *Design for a Brain* Ashby tantalisingly mentions the possibility of constructing a mobile homeostat in a thought experiment, "Suppose U is mobile and is ultrastable, with its critical states set so that it seeks situations of high illumination." The homeostat as demonstrated by Ashby never was mobile and the four variable machine represents within itself both organism and environment, brain and anti-brain together[5]. A mobile homeostat must be configured to interact with its external environment via appropriate transducers.

Like other researchers in this field [6,7,11,13] I have used the Braitenberg vehicle as an idealized platform on which to study the mobile homeostat. In 1984 neuroscientist Valentino Braitenberg published a small but influential book outlining a series of thought experiments that develop simple mobile robots displaying increasingly sophisticated behaviours [5]. Each Braitenberg Vehicle has light sensing eyes and is adapted to its simple environment containing light sources which attract or repel them (phototaxis). Vehicles 1 to 5 develop the concepts of (1) motility; (2) tropisms; (3) excitatory and inhibitory synapses; (4) non-linear activation functions; and (5) recurrent networks. With vehicle 6 we are invited to imagine these vehicles roaming the finite surface of a kitchen tabletop. Vehicles that wander too far from the light source at the centre of their tabletop universe are greeted with a precipitous fall to their doom from whence they are recycled for their parts. Braitenberg considers the possibilities of stochastic and evolutionary approaches to developing vehicles that adapt and survive in this environment.

Franchi's research [11] considers a type 1 Braitenberg Vehicle with a single motor that can run forwards or backwards. This motor is controlled by a single homeostat unit. The robot inhabits a 1-dimensional world that presents a light-gradient to a single cyclopic eye. This single essential variable favours a band of high illumination and consequently the vehicle will eventually come to rest or achieve a dynamic equilibrium (oscillation) within this illuminated region. The independent control of two motors requires at least two homeostat units, one per motor. This vehicle will live in a 2-dimensional plane with the light source at the centre of its world. It is equipped with a pair of directional eyes that can sense its position relative to this light source.

The homeostat realizes a system of variables that represent measurements taken in the environment or within the reacting organism itself. The first step is to identify these variables in the simulation. Starting with the environment the eyes detect the position of the robot relative to a single light source. Physiologically our eyes have a logarithmic response to light that compensates for the fall in intensity due to the inverse square law. Ignoring distance then, each

---

[5] W. Ross Ashby Aphorisms, "Every brain is also an anti-brain".

eye returns the cosine of its angle of incidence to the light source. The output of the eyes is therefore a pair of sine-waves at 90° to each other defining the angular position of the robot relative to the light source. Another variable in the environment is the distance from the light source. As for outputs, within the simulated robot chassis there are two motors, each one connected to a separate unit. As motors can run backwards as well as forwards the speed of the motor is represented by a number in the range [−1, 1]. These two motor variables are the only way in which the robot can act on, or react to, the environment.

The simulated environment is based on a simple kinematic model for 2-wheeled robots [15] where the robot's position and angle are expressed as a function of the left and right motor variables. The robot turns using differential

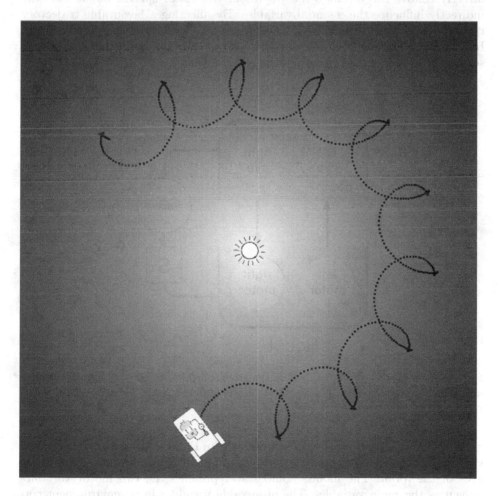

Fig. 2. A simulated mobile homeostat in a 2-dimensional environment with a central source of illumination. The trajectory of an adapted robot is plotted as a series of points.

steering described by a differential equation for the change in angle with respect to time. The robot's velocity is the average of the two wheels so its coordinates change as a function of velocity and angle. We find that a classic 2-unit homeostat is able to adapt to this environment. This is to be expected because it is possible to construct type 2 & 3 Braitenberg vehicles of similar complexity by hand. A wide range of behaviours that achieve stability are possible including straightforward orbital motion and the epicyclic trajectory illustrated in Fig. 2 showing actual output from the simulation.

Ashby's secondary feedback loop acts directly on the variables essential to the survival of the robot, namely the distance from the light source which is inversely correlated with the proximity of the edge of the table. The robot can directly control the variables that represent the motor speeds, but it can only indirectly influence the essential variables. By affecting a favourable trajectory through the world its goal is to bring these essential variables under control. In other words, it can only influence its essential variables and the values of its sensors by acting on them through the environment.

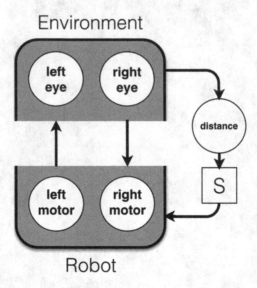

Fig. 3. Secondary feedback loop where the environment acts on essential variables, is necessary for ultrastability. The essential variable influences the behavior of the robot via the step-mechanism S.

The simple sensorimotor loop is illustrated in Fig. 3 as the effect of the motor variables on the environment and the environmental influence of the light on the eyes of the robot. The mobile homeostat represents the two motor variables known as the *main* variables. The observable variables in its environment correspond to its sensors and the variables essential to its survival. All of the main variables in the mobile homeostat have essential limits, but this diagram emphasises the importance of the distance as being essential to its survival. When the distance exceeds a critical value, the equivalent of the edge of Braitenberg's tabletop, the uniselector step-mechanism must be triggered for *all* of the main variables.

The mobile homeostat is configured along the lines of Ashby's machine with input as described in *Introduction to Cybernetics* [3]. Each external input is identified as a parameter. For a set of n internal variables $x_i(1 \leq i \leq n)$ and a set of m external parameters $a_j(1 \leq j \leq m)$ the state-determined system is described[6] as a set of functions as in Eq. 2. The mobile homeostat will have $n = 2$ internal units, one per motor. Each homeostat unit receives input from every other unit including feedback from itself together with an additional $m = 3$ parameters giving each simulated unit $m + n$ inputs.

$$\frac{dx_i}{dt} = f_i(x_1, ..., x_n, a_1, ..., a_m) \tag{2}$$

The architecture of the homeostat, intended as a static demonstrator, does not readily lend itself to being hooked up to essential variables in the environment. Each unit is self-contained such that when its needle goes out of bounds then the relay and uniselector for that unit *only* is activated. The only global control is the frequency at which activation may occur which Ashby judged should be somewhere between 1 and 10 s. Thus the relay mechanism represents the essential variable for a single unit only. There is no obvious mechanism by which uniselectors in multiple units can be activated via a common signal.

Ashby comes to the rescue with his description of the *fully joined system* in which he describes a setup with "three essential variables ...all affected by the environment, and all able to veto the stability of the step-mechanisms S."[7] This many-to-one relationship can only represent a configuration where the essential variables are external parameters to a set of step-mechanisms. In the case of our mobile homeostat a single environmental variable representing the robot's distance from the light source is input to the robot as a parameter, as with the sensor inputs. This creates a channel from this parameter to both of the robot's internal variables by which their stability can be vetoed.

The power of veto can only be ensured if the parametric input from the essential variable remains under manual control. If this were placed under control of the uniselector then it would simply be able to disable the threatening input rather than adapting to it. It would be akin to an organism choosing to ignore pain rather than rectifying the cause of the pain. The veto signal needs to come as a short sharp shock so that it doesn't normally interfere with the stable fields of the internal variables. The distance parameter value is the output of a (Heaviside) function that is 0 when the distance is less than a threshold representing the perimeter and 1 otherwise. This veto signal is sufficient to drive both units into their critical regions causing the uniselectors of each unit to be activated at the point where the mobile homeostat falls off the edge of the world.

---

[6] Design for a Brain, 2nd revised edition, p262.

[7] Figure 11/10/1 Design for a Brain, 2nd revised edition.

2.1 Ultrastability

The first experiment is to verify that the mobile homeostat coupled with this environment produces stable solutions in a reasonable time-scale. Each sample is the number of trials required to achieve a stable solution. The length of a trial is defined to be the time period after which the essential variables are checked for being within their limits. Ashby suggested that essential variables are not checked continuously but perhaps every 3 s or so, the value used for these experiments. Robots that remain stable (with no uniselector events) for a full minute (20 trials) are deemed to be stable solutions (the 20 stable trials are subtracted from the total). Each test contains 100 independent samples initiated at a random position and parameter configuration. The data are merged and ranked so that the mean ranks may be compared.

Table 1. Ultrastability in 2,3,4 variables

Variables	2	3	4
Sample size	100	100	100
Mean rank	23.64	46.12	80.74

Table 1 captures the results for 2, 3, and 4-unit homeostats. We stop at four simply because that's how many units the original homeostat contained, but also the direction the results are headed is plain to see. Each is a fully-joined system such that every unit of the homeostat is fully (and bi-directionally) joined with every other. Firstly, we note that the 2-unit homeostat does indeed produce stable solutions. Ashby's *law of requisite variety* states that a control system need have no more variety than the environment it controls, and this demonstrates that no more than two units are required. Furthermore, he predicted that as we add additional redundant units then the required adaptation time would increase. Given that 2-units are sufficient to control the robot in this environment, in the experiment with 3 and 4 units we would expect to see an increase in the time taken to reach stability.

The results follow a geometric distribution so a non-parametric Kruskal-Wallis analysis of variance (H-test) is used to compare the mean ranks of the three sample sets. Under the null hypothesis the mean ranks of the three sample sets are the same. For at least a 95 % degree of certainty ($alpha = 0.05$) with $k(groups) - 1 = 2$ degrees of freedom the H critical value is 5.991. The H-statistic is calculated to be 197.85 > 5.991 therefore there is a significant difference between the mean ranks of the three groups with varying number of homeostat units (at least two of the sample sets differ). With a mean rank score of 23.64 for 2-units, 46.12 for 3-units, and 80.74 for 3-units, this indicates that the time taken to reach stability increases with the number of (redundant) units.

3   Reducing Connectivity

Ashby observed that while the fully joined system retains generality it would be an impractical solution in reality. Real organisms exploit constraint in the world by limiting their own internal connectivity where it is not needed. First and foremost this is a property of the environment. Only if there are real constraints in the world can the homeostat exploit this by reducing its own internal connectivity.

The diagram of immediate effects for the simulated environment is illustrated in Fig. 4. This captures additional variables that are part of the simulated environment but are not parameters to the robot (The set of $m + n$ function parameters). For example the robot cannot directly sense its absolute position nor absolute angle. The left and right motor values are the two main variables of the robot and are parameters (square boxes) of the environment, while the distance, left and right eyes are input parameters to the robot. There is considerable constraint in this environment. For example the values of the eyes are independent of the distance given the position of the robot.

Ashby's counter-intuitive thesis is that "coordination can take place through the environment; communication within the nervous system is not always necessary." This can be tested in the mobile homeostat by severing all connections between the two halves of the 2-unit homeostat brain. Both units still receive all the available input parameters and their recurrent inputs. This is achieved in the homeostat by switching just those severed connections to manual control and setting their weights to zero. The effect of this is to reduce the variety of the system towards that of the environment.

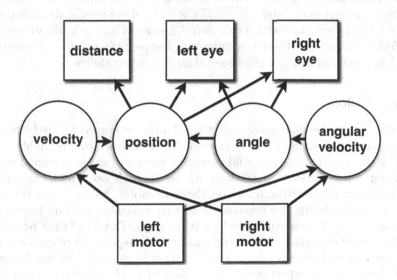

Fig. 4. Diagram of immediate effects showing constraint among environmental variables (circles) and parameters to/from the homeostat (squares).

If this is a cut too far then there will be no stable solutions. However, the hard-wired neural circuits of Braitenberg's Vehicles 2 and 3, with crossed and uncrossed channels between eye and motor but no lateral communication, demonstrate the workability of low-connectivity adaptations in this environment. The mobile homeostat with disjoint variables includes this space of simpler vehicles while excluding more complex models with internally recurrent networks. There is *no direct connection* between the two main variables of the disjoint homeostat, but they may still influence each other indirectly through the environment.

Table 2. Ultrastability in 2 variables with varying connectivity

Variables	2 (disjoint)	2 (fully joined)
Sample size	100	100
Mean rank	37.27	63.23

The data for the system of two fully-joined (bidirectionally connected) variables from above is compared with a system of two internally disjoint variables. The results are shown in Table 2. To compare the two sample sets both with 2-units but with different internal connectivities, a non-parametric Mann-Whitney (U-test) for large sample sizes is used to determine whether the two samples are drawn from different populations. Under the null hypothesis the mean ranks of the two sample sets are the same. A one tailed test is used because the time taken to reach stability is expected to increase with the number of units. For a 95 % degree of certainty (*alpha* = 0.05) the critical value of Z for a one-tailed test is -1.645. In this case with a calculated Z score of $6.34 > 1.645$ we can state with 95 % certainty that there is a difference between the two groups. Reducing internal connectivity reduces the time taken to reach stability.

3.1   Discussion

While these experiments demonstrate that the classic homeostat architecture is able to control a robot with two degrees-of-freedom they also highlight a shortcoming in the way that the essential variables are connected to the environment. The distance *veto* must be artificially forced through both main variables in order to trigger the essential limits on those variables. Ashby noted this weakness in his journal, "In the homeostat, further variables are put between the environment and the essential variables (the relay). The relay thus never 'sees' the environment directly."[8] This arrangement is the equivalent of growing a protective shell around the essential variables rather than employing intelligence to avoid a threat. Ashby experimented with eliminating this one-to-one connection

---

[8] W. Ross Ashby journals, vol.12, p2960, August 1950.

between the main and essential variables in the homeostat[9] by switching out the relays and placing the uniselectors under manual control.

Experiments with decoupling the essential variables from the main variables serve to highlight another early postulate of Ashby, the *equivalence of levels*, "all levels are equivalent for the formulation of the general laws of psychology"[10]. In decoupling the essential variables from the motor variables and slaving them only to the essential variable representing distance, the unintended consequence is that these variables inevitably get stuck at saturation (full forward or full reverse). These stuck variables create a wall of constancy that render the robot unreactive. The conclusion is that homeostasis is indeed necessary at all levels from individual internal variables to essential variables directly observed in the environment.

A theory of how the essential variables might be re-connected did not begin to emerge until the design of the DAMS (Dispersive and Multistable System) putting it beyond the scope of this paper. According to Ashby, "This picture must be used if any severe test of a reacting system (artificial brain) is to be applied."[11]

3.2   Conclusion

This research extends previous work in applying the classic homeostat architecture to the problem of controlling a robot in a simulated two-dimensional environment with two degrees-of-freedom. This is inspired by Ashby's thought experiment of a mobile homeostat seeking situations of high-illumination. This experimental setup allowed us to explore the principle of *ultrastability*, Ashby's *law of requisite variety*, and the effects of increasing the number of units or decreasing connectivity. The next steps will be to explore the potential for social interaction between multiple mobile homeostats and also to validate these simulations by embedding the homeostat within a physical robot. In the words of Ashby, "How will it end? I suggest that the simplest way to find out is to make the thing and see." [1].

A   Appendix: MATLAB Model for Fig. 1

```
function i = inputs1(t)
# return a row vector of inputs over time (deflection)
# deflection at D1, D2
if ((50<t && t<55) || (150<t && t<155))
    i = [0.3];
else
    i = [0.2];
```

---

[9] W. Ross Ashby journals, vol.12, p2748, February 1950.
[10] W. Ross Ashby journals, vol.1, p40, 1928.
[11] W. Ross Ashby journals, vol.12, p2962, August 1950.

```
  endif
endfunction

function w = weights1(t)
  if (t<100)
    # three rows: unit 1 output; unit 2 output; deflection
    # two columns: unit 1 input, unit 2 input (manually
        controlled)
    # each unit has fixed negative feedback −0.5
    # initial 1−>2 weighting −0.1 reversed at R1
    # deflection effects unit 2 with weight 1.0
    w = [−0.5, −0.1; 1.0, −0.5; 0.0, 1.0 ];
  elseif (t<110)
    # reverse commutator on input to 2nd unit (1−>2) at R1
    w = [−0.5, +0.1; 1.0, −0.5; 0.0, 1.0 ];
  else
    # uniselector selects new weights on 1st unit (2−>1)
        post R1
    w = [−0.5, +0.1; −0.668, −0.5; 0.0, 1.0 ];
  endif
endfunction

function xdot = h1(x,t)
  h = 1.0; j = 1.0;
  # multiply inputs by weights, a
  xa = [x(1:2)',inputs1(t)]*weights1(t);
  # output (xdot) represents x1, x2, x1', x2'
  xdot(1) = x(3);
  xdot(2) = x(4);
  xdot(3) = h*xa(1) − j*x(3);
  xdot(4) = h*xa(2) − j*x(4);
endfunction

t=linspace(0,200,1000)
x0 = [0;0;0;0]
x = lsode("h1",x0,t)
plot(t,x(:,1),"−;unit 1;k",t,x(:,2),":;unit 2;k");
```

References

1. Ross Ashby, W.: The electronic brain. Radio Electron. **XX**(6), 77–79 (1949)
2. Ross Ashby, W.: Design for a Brain. Chapman & Hall, London (1952)
3. Ross Ashby, W.: An Introduction to Cybernetics. Chapman & Hall, London (1956)
4. Boden, M.: Mind as Machine: A History of Cognitive Science. Clarendon Press, Oxford (2006)

 5. Braitenberg, V.: Vehicles: Experiments in Synthetic Psychology. MIT Press, Cambridge (1984)
 6. Di Paolo, E.A.: Homeostatic adaptation to inversion of the visual field and other sensorimotor disruptions (2000)
 7. Di Paolo, E.A.: Organismically-inspired robotics: homeostatic adaptation and teleology beyond the closed sensorimotor loop. In: Murase, K., Asakura, T. (eds.) Dynamical Systems Approaches to Embodiment and Sociality. Advanced Knowledge International, Adelaide (2003)
 8. Eldridge, A.: Ashby's Homeostat in Simulation (2002, unpublished). http://www.ecila.org/ecila_files/content/papers/ACEhom.pdf
 9. Ross Ashby, W.: Homeostasis, cybernetics: circular causal and feedback mechanisms in biological and social systems. In: Foerster, H. (ed.) Transactions of the Ninth Conference. Josiah Macy, Jr. Foundation (1952)
10. Franchi, S.: Life, death, and resurrection of the homeostat. In: European Meeting of the Computing and Philosophy Association (E-Cap), Barcelona, Spain (2009)
11. Franchi, S.: Homeostats for the 21st century? simulating ashby simulating the brain. Second-Order Dynamics (2014)
12. Freud, S.: Project for a scientific psychology. In: (Masson, J.M. (ed.) and Trans.) The Complete Letters of Sigmund Freud to Wilhelm Fliess, 1887–1904. Belknap Press of Harvard University Press, Cambridge (1985)
13. Michael Herrmann, J., Holicki, M., Der, R.: On Ashbys homeostat: a formal model of adaptive regulation. In: From animals to animats 8: Proceedings of the Eighth International Conference on the Simulation of Adaptive Behavior, pp. 324–333 (2004)
14. Husbands, P., Holland, O.: The ratio club: a hub of british cybernetics. In: Husbands, Holland, Wheeler (eds.) The Mechanical Mind in History. MIT Press (2008)
15. Lucas, G.W.: An elementary model for the differential steering system of robot actuators. The Rossum Project (2000). http://rossum.sourceforge.net/papers/DiffSteer/DiffSteer.html
16. GreyWalter, W.: The Living Brain. G. Duckworth, London (1953)

Multi-Robot Coverage: A Bee Pheromone Signalling Approach

Ipek Caliskanelli[✉], Bastian Broecker, and Karl Tuyls

Department of Computer Science, University of Liverpool, Liverpool, UK
{ipek.caliskanelli,bastian.broecker,k.tuyls}@liverpool.ac.uk

Abstract. In this paper we propose **BeePCo**, a multi-robot coverage approach based on honey bee colony behaviour. Specifically, we propose a honey bee inspired pheromone signalling method that allows a team of robots to maximise the total area covered in an environment in a distributed manner. The effectiveness of the proposed algorithm is experimentally evaluated on three different sizes of multi robot systems (MRSs) and compared against an ant-inspired coverage algorithm (StiCo) to show the different characteristics of these two approaches.

Keywords: Multi-robot systems · Bio-inspired · Bee-inspired · Coverage

1 Introduction

Recent years have seen a rapidly growing interest in multi-robot systems for automatically surveilling environments of different size, type and complexity. Multi-robot systems (MRS) consist of multiple interacting robots, each executing an application-specific control strategy, which is not centrally steered. The interest in MRS for surveillance is largely motivated by the wide range of application areas including the protection of safety-critical technical infrastructures and buildings, search and rescue scenarios, the monitoring of danger zones which cannot be entered by humans, for instance, in the case of a nuclear incident, a bio-hazard, etc. As such automated surveillance has become a well studied topic in multi-robot research with a strong practical relevance.

A key advantage of robot-based surveillance lies in its flexibility achieved through possible positional changes of the robots, which makes this form also suited for surveillance applications in unknown or complex environments. In contrast to stationary wireless sensor-based surveillance systems or networks, however, robot-based surveillance systems have not yet found their way to real-world applications on a broader scale. Two interrelated key components of every multi-robot surveillance system are exploration and coverage of a potentially unknown environments. The term *exploration* refers to the discovery of all traversable regions of the environment through one or several robots [30]. The term *coverage* refers to the maximisation of (or the process of maximising) the total area covered by the sensors of the involved robot(s) [30].

© Springer International Publishing Switzerland 2015
C.J. Headleand et al. (Eds.): ALIA 2014, CCIS 519, pp. 124–140, 2015.
DOI: 10.1007/978-3-319-18084-7_10

Previously, we have investigated three different biological inspirations: the stigmergy principle of ants, the foraging behaviour of honey bee colonies and the pheromone signalling procedure of honey bees. *StiCo*, the stigmergy principle, is based on the observations of ant colonies, and is used as a coordination mechanism for coverage by multi-robot systems [30]. The foraging behaviour of honey bee colonies [24] are inspected and used to solve robot coordination, navigation and path planning issues in multi-robot platforms. *PS* [7], a honey bee inspired pheromone signalling procedure, is used to address load balancing and redundancy control issues in wireless sensor networks.

In this paper we are concerned with coverage issues of multi-robot systems. Specifically we explore the performance outcomes of the bees *pheromone signalling* procedure, which we call *BeePCo*, when applied to the coverage problem in multi-robot systems. The proposed *BeePCo* mechanism is inspired by biological processes: how social insects (bees) control and orchestrate with other members of a hive [1, 2]. As abstract agents, individual bees have many similarities with robots (as do bee colonies with MRSs). The required similarities are in terms of individual wellbeing (bee/robot) and collective welfare (colony/MRS). With our approach, we enable group coordination among robots, where the individual movement-related decisions of each robot is based on its local information. The proposed approach is evaluated in simulation against the well-known ant algorithm, *StiCo* [30].

The remainder of this paper is structured as follows. Section 2 reviews the related work in the areas of multi-agent coverage and bio-inspired techniques in networked distributed systems. Section 3 covers pheromone signalling based coverage algorithms for MRSs together with the required biological background. The paper continues with the experimental setup and results in Sect. 4. We conclude in Sect. 5.

2   Related Work

This section gives an overview of relevant literature that has attempted to describe, analyse, or efficiently exploit bio-inspired techniques for addressing the multi-agent coverage problem. This section is split into two main parts of the problem targeted in this research: Sect. 2.1 provides examples of existence work in the fields of multi-agent coverage in MRSs, whereas Sect. 2.2 shows the significant bio-inspired research work in the field of networked distributed systems in general.

2.1   Multi Robot Coverage

The concept of coverage as a metric for evaluating robotic systems which was first introduced by Gage [13]. Gage defines three basic types of coverage: blanket coverage, where its objective is to achieve a node formation which maximises the total detection area; barrier coverage, which aims to minimise the probability of undetected intrusion through the barrier; and sweep- or repetitive-coverage with the goal to cover all accessible interest points in a given environment over time, while maximising the rate of visits over all points and minimising the total distance travelled by all robots.

Blanket coverage is most common for the deployment of mobile sensor networks in an unknown environment; the sensor nodes are initially placed in a compact configuration, and the nodes try to spread out to maximise the area covered by the network. One example for such a use case is a hazardous material leak in a damaged structure. Mobile sensor nodes equipped with chemical sensors spread out from a initial position to gather information about location and concentration of the hazard. Due to the fact that the communication infrastructure could be damaged, the nodes have to ensure their own network structure even if single nodes get lost or destroyed. Many approaches in this field are based on the potential field technique first introduced by Khatib [22].

Barrier and repetitive-coverage problems originate from the computational geometry *Art Gallery Problem* [10] and its variant for mobile guard for mobile guards, the *Watchman Route Problem* [25]. *Barrier coverage* is the problem of placing sensors (of robots) to act as guards to protect a region from being entered by an intruder and often used in randomly deployed military applications [23]. In robotics, *repetitive-coverage* can be described as a problem where a team of robots has to visit multiple *points of interests* (POI) in a known environment frequently, to perform certain tasks. The goal of such algorithms is to keep the average visit frequency over all POIs high, while achieving a minimal total travelled distance and a balanced workload over all robots. Typical real world use cases for such problems are patrolling, lawn mowing and cleaning up chemical spills. Many approaches concerning multi-robot patrol partition the area into sub-areas divided between the robots. Inside such a sub-area, each robot applies a single robot patrol algorithm. Ahmadi and Stone [1] describe a negotiation-based approach for distributing the area between the robots and dealing with events such as addition or removal of robots to the environment. Jung and Sukhatme [19] introduce a region based approach for tracking targets in a system with mobile robots and stationary sensors.

Another important form of multi-robot coverage is *terrain coverage* or multi-robot exploration. It can be defined as a problem where a robot tries to visit each and every location in a continuous bounded unknown environment by avoiding obstacles and perform defined tasks [8,12,26]. A terrain coverage algorithm must generate a coverage path, which is a chain of motion steps for a robot, the optimal coverage path takes minimal time and guarantee to cover the entire terrain and perform the task efficiently.

Many approaches divide the environment into grid cells and explore one cell at the time until the whole area is covered. One of the first approaches was Spanning Tree Coverage (STC) which solves single robot coverage optimistically [11]. The same idea was applied by Hazon and Kaminka on a multi-robot system [17].

Batalin et al. propose a multi-robot algorithm, which spread the robots in the terrain and makes them avoid each others sensing area [3].

Several authors propose marked based approaches in multi-robot exploration, in which robots make bids on a sub-task of an exploration attempted [35,38]. These bids are based on values such as expected information gain and travelled cost to a particular location. This approach seems to minimise the costs while maximising the benefit.

2.2 Bio-inspired Solutions

Bio-inspired solutions are often used to solve complex problems (e.g. MAC level routing, load balancing, task allocation and resource scheduling, network coverage, and emergence) in the broad research area of distributed systems with a particular interest on wireless sensor networks, many and multicore systems, swarm intelligence and multi-robot systems to make systems more reliable, efficient and self-organised. Ant colony optimisation, bee colony optimisation and artificial immune systems are three of the most commonly used biological inspirations.

Based on the observation of the collective foraging behaviour of ants, many research studies are held on **Ant Colony Optimisation (ACO)** on the ability of ants to converge on the shortest path from their nest to a food source to improve energy efficiency and QoS in routing. ARA [15], AntHocNet [9], ARO [37] and *StiCo* [30] can be listed as some of the key research in ACO.

Conforming to this swarm metaphor, **Bee Colony Optimisation (BCO)** was introduced by Karaboga et al. [20,21]. Scientists are inspired by variety of different behaviours of bees: foraging behaviour in Lemmens et al. [24], Beehive protocol [36], BeeSensor [31]; bees mating procedure in [29,34]; pheromone signalling mechanism in PS [7].

Artificial Immune Systems (AIS) are inspired by the human/ mammalian immune system. Sensitivity to detecting environmental change, and identifying the foreign/infectious agents is used, particularly for security purposes in anomaly detections. SASHA [4], DSR [32,33], DNRS [2] are some of the significant research in the field of autonomous distributed systems inspired by AIS.

BTMS [16] uses zygote differentiation to extend the network lifetime whilst speeding up task mapping and scheduling. Homogeneous nodes begin in a default state and within time nodes differentiate themselves dynamically to perform distinct tasks according to their location.

In our previous work, pheromone signalling based load-balancing, *PS* [5,7], we present a dynamic technique for Wireless Sensor Networks (WSNs) that is applied at run time at the application layer. *PS* is inspired from the pheromone signalling mechanism found in bees and provides distributed WSN control that uses local information only. *PS* is unique; unlike many load balancing approaches are applied at link or network layer [14,18,36] and balance only communication load, *PS* is an application-layer protocol and manages both computation and communication load. In [6], we extend our initial *PS* technique by introducing additional network elements in the form of robotic vehicles for Wireless Sensor and Robot Networks (WSRNs). We merge different subclasses of cyber-physical systems (sensors and robots) together to increase the area coverage *effectively*, which directly increases the service availability and extends the network lifetime by benefiting from their heterogeneity. *Effective* area coverage in this research is defined as achieving the highest service availability while minimising movement to conserve energy. To achieve the desired effective area coverage, we have extended our *PS* technique to guide robots towards the areas of the sensor field where the sensor nodes have run out of battery and are unable to provide service. The same pheromone signalling process is applied into multi-robot systems in this research and explained in detail in the next section.

3   Pheromone Signalling Based Coverage Technique

We describe our previous work on a pheromone signalling algorithm which is applied to the WSN domain. Unlike our previous work on WSNs, this paper focuses on applying the pheromone signalling technique to MRSs. WSNs and MRSs have different application requirements, and in order to indicate the application domain we change the name of the pheromone signalling technique (from *PS* for WSNs) to *BeePCo* for MRSs. The bee-inspired coverage algorithm, *BeePCo*, described in this section is a completely decentralised approach that has low computational overhead and direct local communication.

Changes in pheromone levels are used by many social animals to orchestrate the colony by assigning responsibilities to each individual. Roberts [28] explains the process of larvae differentiation in beehives as an example of such orchestration. Bees have developed a special hormonal system to ensure every beehive has a queen, which maintains the stability of the colony and orchestrates the behaviour of all other bees. Throughout its life, a queen bee stimulates a pheromone called Queen Mandibular Pheromone (QMP), which makes the worker bees aware of its presence as queen. This hormonal mechanism works as follows: the worker bees lick the queen bee and pass the pheromone to the others. If there is no pheromone passed through the worker bees, they will then consider the queen as dead. In that case, workers will select a larva to be fed with large amounts of the royalactin protein. That protein induces the differentiation of honey bee larvae into a queen. If worker bees keep receiving the pheromone, they will be aware that there is a queen bee to orchestrate the colony and will take no action towards building a new queen.

The proposed coverage technique is inspired by the behaviour described above. The role of a queen bee denotes a robot that is responsible for managing the execution of all service requests it receives. Throughout this paper we will refer these robots as Queen Robots (QR) and their responsibility (service) is to patrol an unknown area. The basic strategy of the algorithm is based on the periodic transmission of pheromone by QRs, and its retransmission by recipients to their neighbours. The pheromone level of each robot decays with time and with distance to the source. All robots accumulate pheromone received from other QRs and if at a particular time the pheromone level of a robot is below a given threshold this robot will differentiate itself into a QR. To make it clear, the threshold we used for this work is 10,000 for this paper - a very high value, which means all the robots are assigned to be QRs and they remain as QRs until they run out of energy. Although we do not particularly benefit from robot differentiation for this work, we still describe the differentiation process for the completeness of this work and to provide a base for our future work. In the *BeePCo* technique, the level of pheromone indicates how well a certain area is covered. Areas in the robotic arena that have lower level of pheromone, at a given time, demonstrate a lower robot density as opposed to other parts. This means, areas with low pheromone level have either low coverage or are not covered at all.

The proposed *BeePCo* algorithm consists of four parts which are executed on every robot of the MRS: two of them are time-triggered (differentiation cycle and decay of pheromone), whereas the other two (propagation of received pheromone and robotic move) occur together in a single event-triggered process. The first time-triggered part, referred to as the differentiation cycle (Algorithm 1), is executed by every robot of the MRS every T_{QR} time units. On each execution, each robot checks its current pheromone level h_i against a predefined level $threshold_{QR}$. We set the $threshold_{QR}$ to 10,000 for this paper - a level unreachable in practice - which means all of the differentiate into QRs and remain as QRs until they run out of energy. QRs transmits pheromone to its network neighbourhood to make its presence felt. Each pheromone dose hd is represented as a two-position vector. The first element of the vector denotes the distance in hops to the QR that has produced it (and therefore is initialised as 0 in line 4 of Algorithm 1). The second element is the actual dosage of the pheromone that will be absorbed by the neighbours.

Algorithm 1. Differentiation Cycle

1: every T_{QR} do
2: if $(h_i < threshold_{QR})$ **then**
3:     QR_i = true
4:     broadcast $hd = \{0, h_{QR}\}$
5: **else**
6:     $QR_i = false$
7: **end if**

The event-triggered part of *BeePCo* deals with the propagation of the pheromone released by QRs (as described above in the differentiation cycle) and received at neighbouring robots. The purpose of propagation is to extend the influence of QRs to their surroundings (neighbouring robots in the communication range). Propagation is not a periodic activity, and happens every time a robot receives a pheromone dose. The pseudocode given in Algorithm 2. Upon receiving a pheromone dose, a robot checks whether the transmitting QR is located sufficiently near for the pheromone to be effective. It does that by comparing the first element of hd with a predefined $threshold_{hopcount}$. If the hd has travelled more hops than the $threshold_{hopcount}$, the robot simply discards it. If not, it adds the received dosage of the pheromone to its own pheromone level h_i and propagates the pheromone to its neighbourhood. Before forwarding it, the robot updates the hd vector element by incrementing the hop count, and by multiplying the dosage by a decay factor $0 < K_{HOPDECAY} < 1$. This represents pheromone transmission decaying with distance from the source. Once the pheromones are propagated, a move cycle is triggered. As well as the propagation cycle, move cycle also occurs when a robot receives pheromones. The move cycle illustrates the general movement behaviour of a robot as given in Algorithm 3.

Algorithm 2. Pheromone Propagation Cycle

1: **while** hd is received **do**
2:    **if** $(hd[1] < threshold_{hopcount})$ **then**
3:       $h_i = h_i + hd[2]$
4:       broadcast $hd = \{hd[1] + 1, hd[2].K_{HOPDECAY}\}$
5:    **else**
6:       drop hd
7:    **end if**
8:    go to BeePCo Move Cycle
9: **end while**

Algorithm 3. Move Cycle

1: **if** (pheromone received) **then**
2:    PS-guided moving decision
3: **else**
4:    keep moving in the direction of the last move
5:    broadcast communication link request
6:    establish local communication links
7: **end if**

If a robot receives pheromone it makes the decision of where to move by selecting a target destination in the opposite direction of the received pheromone, based on *BeePCo*. The moving decision of robots are based on vector addition and its pseudo code appears in Algorithm 4. Given the robot's movement behaviour and assuming that all robots know their location, we calculate the angle of the received pheromone with the use of the sender's x and y coordinates. To do this, we resolve the horizontal and vertical components based on the amount of received pheromone level, h_i, and the coordinates of the QRs. In order to find the magnitude, we sum up all the horizontal and vertical components. In order to determine the direction of the magnitude, we take the arctangent of the magnitude and resolve x and y coordinates. This process happens on-demand as the robotic agents receive pheromone from as part of propagation cycle.

Algorithm 4. Moving Decision

1: **if** $(h_i > 0)$ **then**
2:    **for** all the received pheromones (p) of the robot **do**
3:       $diff_X = p_{Sender_X} - currentCoordinate_X$
4:       $diff_Y = p_{Sender_Y} - currentCoordinate_Y$
5:       $\theta = ArcTangentQuadrant(diff_Y, diff_X)$
6:       $component_X = p.hd * \cos\theta$
7:       $component_Y = p.hd * \sin\theta$
8:       $Sum_X + = component_X$
9:       $Sum_Y + = component_Y$
10:   **end for**
11: **end if**
12: $magnitude = \sqrt{Sum_X{}^2 + Sum_Y{}^2}$
13: $\theta_{destination} = ArcTangentQuadrant(Sum_Y, Sum_X)$
14: apply 180 degrees shift to $\theta_{destination}$
15: clear all received pheromones

If a robot does not receive any pheromone at its destination location, it surveils this position provided it does not receive any new pheromone. This happens when robots are not in each others' communication ranges (when they cannot receive pheromones from each other) and allows them to spread out in the area.

The second time-triggered part of the algorithm, shown in Algorithm 5 is a simple periodic decay of the pheromone level of each robot. Every T_{DECAY} time units, h_i is multiplied by a decay factor $0 < K_{TIMEDECAY} < 1$ to indicate reduced pheromone levels due to elapsed time.

Algorithm 5. Decay Cycle

1: **for** every T_{DECAY} **do**
2:   $h_i = h_i.K_{TIMEDECAY}$
3: **end for**

Although decay and differentiation cycles have zero effect on the coverage presented in this paper, we have explicitly formalised and explained them to establish a ground for our future work and for the completeness of this research. In our future work, we will build up on these cycles and use our approach to control redundant processing and task executions as well as coverage issues in MRSs.

4 Evaluation Environment and Experimental Results

To evaluate the effectiveness of *BeePCo* at providing network coverage, and to establish a valid comparison between *StiCo* and *BeePCo*, we apply both algorithms on the simulation platform that *StiCo* is developed on. For further details about the simulation framework, we refer to [27].

The experimental work presented in this section aims to show the area coverage of the *BeePCo* and *StiCo* techniques. Area coverage in this study is defined as maximising the total area covered by the sensors of the robot(s), as defined in [30]. The algorithms are applied on a MSR of 20, 30 and 40 robots, each having a sensing and communication radius of 25 cm (simulating *E-puck* robots). The application arena size is set to 300 cm × 300 cm, and the robots are initially deployed randomly in the centre of the arena, in a square 5 cm × 5 cm region. We evaluate the three following scenarios:

- **BeePCo** represents a case where a wide spread of the robots in the arena is based on bees pheromone signalling mechanism. Parameters for the algorithm is $T_{DECAY} = 0.5$ sec, $T_{QR} = 0.066$ sec, and $threshold_{QR} = 10,000$.
- **StiCo** represents a case where the wide spread of the robots in the arena is based on ants stigmergy principle [27].
- **MaxCo** represents the optimal case where the robots' transmission range does not intersect with each other. This scenario is a benchmark for the maximum possible coverage of deployed robots with zero surveillance area overlap within a 300 cm × 300 cm arena. This can also be referred to as potential coverage.

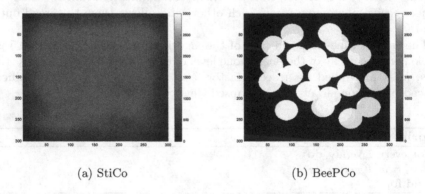

(a) StiCo   (b) BeePCo

Fig. 1. The distribution of robots in the arena using a MRS of 20 robots on StiCo and BeePCo techniques.

Figures 1, 2 and 3 illustrate how evenly the area is covered over time, using 20, 30 and 40 robots on a single run. The colour scale used for Figs. 1, 2, and 3 is from dark to light: uncovered areas are represented in black and the lighter the colour of an area, the higher the percentage of the area being covered over the total time of the experiment. The more evenly the total area is coloured, the more uniform is the distribution of the robots positions over time. These three figures do not only show the performance of the *StiCo* and *BeePCo* approaches, but also illustrates the effects of the number of the robots on the eventual coverage, i.e., more robots improve the performance. The improvement on area coverage using *StiCo* can clearly be seen in Figs. 1a, 2a, and 3a incrementally.

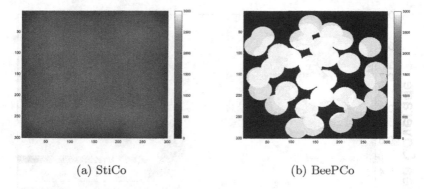

(a) StiCo   (b) BeePCo

Fig. 2. The distribution of robots in the arena using a MRS of 30 robots on StiCo and BeePCo techniques.

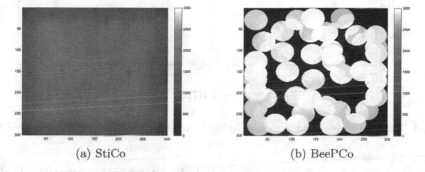

(a) StiCo   (b) BeePCo

Fig. 3. The distribution of robots in the arena using a MRS of 40 robots on StiCo and BeePCo techniques.

Although it is slightly more difficult to see the same effect on *BeePCo*, Figs. 1b, 2b and 3b exhibit the same behaviour. The continuous rotation of *StiCo* enables an uniform distributed coverage in all three figures. On the other hand, the area coverage of *BeePCo* is non-uniform and mainly cluttered in the middle of the arena. This is due to the disconnected communication links. As the robots send pheromone in *BeePCo*, they push each other away until they are no longer connected to the network. Therefore, *BeePCo* is applied on a single robot as long as it possesses communication links to other robots. Once the communication links are no longer available, robots do not move in the *BeePCo* until they establish new connections, otherwise, they remain on their positions until they run out of battery.

Figures 4, 5, 6 and 7 are averaged over 30 independent runs to ensure statistical significance of the results on area coverage. Figure 4 illustrates the experimental results of a MRS with 20 robots comparing the performance of the *StiCo*, *BeePCo* and *MaxCo* approaches against each other in terms of the percentage of area coverage. As shown in Fig. 4, the *StiCo* approach initially spreads the robots faster than *BeePCo* and converges faster. In the *BeePCo* approach, the

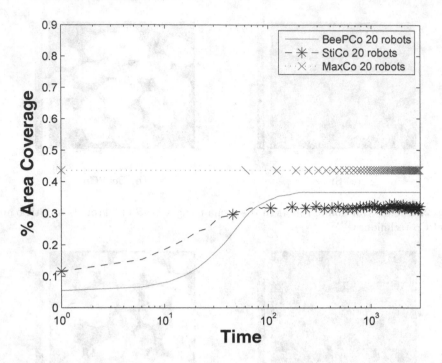

Fig. 4. The percentage of area coverage using MRSs with 20 robots: StiCo and BeePCo.

robots stop spreading after communication links with the other robots are broken because they are outside of the inter-robot transmission range.

Similarly, Fig. 5 illustrates the experimental results on a MRS with 30 robots and compares the performance of the *StiCo, BeePCo* and *MaxCo* approaches against each in terms of the percentage of area coverage. Results show that *BeePCo* achieves better area coverage than *StiCo* technique whilst encouraging not moving once the communication network is lost. This feature of *BeePCo* prevents the algorithm from achieving a more evenly covered area as we explained previously in Fig. 2.

Figure 6 exhibits the experimental results on a MRS with 40 robots and compares the performance of the *StiCo, BeePCo* and *MaxCo* approaches against each in terms of the percentage of area coverage as well as previous figures. In this set of experiments with 40 robots, we also observe the same behaviour: *BeePCo* achieves higher area coverage than the *StiCo* technique through out the simulation time although it does not allow robots to move once the communication network is lost.

In Fig. 7, the *StiCo* and *BeePCo* algorithms are compared against each other with respect to area coverage using 20, 30 and 40 robots. *MaxCo* illustrates the maximum possible area coverage that can be achieved using 20, 30 or 40 robots. These are plotted to show the effectiveness of the *StiCo* and *BeePCo* algorithms in comparison to the maximum possible coverage.

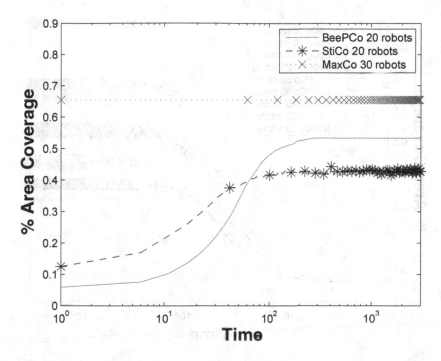

Fig. 5. The percentage of area coverage using MRSs with 30 robots: StiCo and BeePCo.

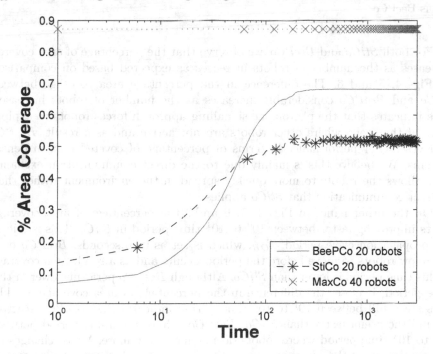

Fig. 6. The percentage of area coverage using MRSs with 40 robots: StiCo and BeePCo.

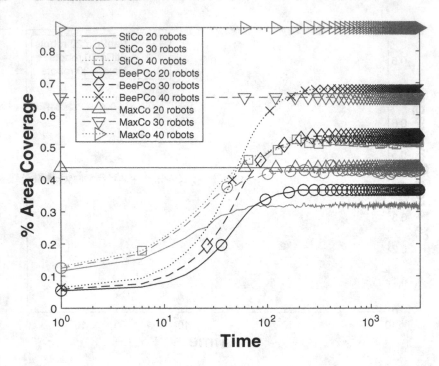

Fig. 7. The percentage of area coverage using MRSs with 20, 30 and 40 robots: StiCo versus BeePCo

For both *StiCo* and *BeePCo*, we observe that the percentage of area covered increases as the number of robots increases as expected based on comparison on Figs. 4, 5 and 6. The difference in the percentage area coverage between *StiCo* and *BeePCo* considerably increases as the number of robots increases. This indicates that the pheromone signalling approach forces robots to explore more of the arena where other robots are not active and as a result, *BeePCo* achieves higher performance in terms of percentage of covered area in denser systems. We believe this is mainly due to the direct communication exchange as it allows the robots to more quickly spread in the environment rather than indirect communication that *StiCo* applies.

On the other hand, in Figs. 4, 5, 6 and 7 the percentage of area coverage starts improving faster between 10^0 to 10^1 time period in *StiCo*. This is due to the propagation cycle period, T_{QR}, which is set as 0.06 seconds. *BeePCo* does not allow robots to move before the period occurs and as a result area coverage in this time period is lower than *StiCo*. Although *BeePCo* performs lower in this time period, it closes the difference in the percentage of area coverage quickly. This steep hill between 10^1 to 10^2 time period indicates that *BeePCo* scatters around the arena faster than *StiCo*. *BeePCo* achieves a stable period between 10^2 to 10^3 time period where robots do not move any more. Minor changes on the percentage of the coverage area in *StiCo* indicates that once the robots are scattered around they keep being scattered around and not getting cluttered after a certain time, which indicates a high stability in this approach too.

5 Conclusions

This paper had two major goals: providing a novel bee-inspired algorithm to address the coverage problem in MRSs (*BeePCo*), and evaluating the different performances and properties of *BeePCo* and *StiCo* in different scenarios. In this paper, we have described a bee-inspired robot guidance technique, *BeePCo* in an attempt to address multi-robot coverage problem. The multi-robot coordination and coverage is a complicated problem in itself, especially when the capacity of robots are limited. As all communications between the robots are through the wireless medium, it is essential to manage the robot coordination with a computationally lightweight algorithm that consumes less energy. Therefore, we propose to improve multi-robot coverage by guiding the robots towards the areas where the robot density is low with the use of bees pheromone signalling algorithm. Simulated experimental results on three different scales of such systems demonstrate that our proposed *BeePCo* technique encourages robots to spread apart from each other using the pheromone signalling process.

Moreover, we have compared our proposed bee-inspired pheromone signalling algorithm (*BeePCo*) against an ant-inspired stigmergic principle (*StiCo*) to show how these bio-inspired behaviours affect coverage on MRSs. Experimental results show that the *StiCo* approach starts spreading the robots as soon as they are deployed. On the other hand, in *BeePCo*, robots start spreading once the periodic cycles occur and therefore takes longer than *StiCo*. In *BeePCo* robots continue expanding the coverage until the robots have moved apart from each other that the communication links are no longer exist, whereas in *StiCo* robots keep moving until they run out of energy. The current *BeePCo* approach fails to improve coverage and remains static when the robots are further apart from each other as this approach requires direct packet exchange based on the local network. This results in uncovered areas in the arena as marked with black in Figs. 1, 2 and 3. The *StiCo* move strategy is based on the indirect pheromone communication and allows robots to explore the arena excessively.

Based on the simulated experiments in this paper, *BeePCo* needs to be improved to decrease the uncovered areas of the arena. We believe merging the advantages of *BeePCo* and *StiCo* may solve the MRS coverage problem which for now remains as future work. In the future, we would also like to consider the resource limitations of the robots, examining the trade off between the total distance taken by a robot and the total service availability of the MRS. From our experience in pheromone signalling algorithm on WSNs, the *BeePCo* algorithm can be applied to MRSs for redundancy control on top of the current coverage and connectivity procedure in a multi-objective manner. It can be easily inferred from the *BeePCo* differentiation cycle that each robot makes its own decision on whether and when it becomes a QR by referring to local information only: its own pheromone level h_i. Although, for this paper we have allowed all robots to be

QRs by setting the predefined $threshold_{QR}$ to 10000, that is done only to focus the single objective: to tackle multi-robot coverage problem. In future, we would like to inspect the MRSs behaviour when $threshold_{QR}$ is set to a lower and more appropriate number to actually enable robot differentiation. This should allow for highly self-organised behaviour which fits the requirements for high-density networked MRSs.

References

1. Ahmadi, M., Stone, P.: A multi-robot system for continuous area sweeping tasks. In: Proceedings of the IEEE International Conference on Robotics and Automation, pp. 1724–1729, May 2006
2. Atakan, B., Akan, O.B.: Immune system based distributed node and rate selection in wireless sensor networks. In: 1st International Conference Bio-Inspired Models of Network, Information and Computing Systems, pp. 1–8, December 2006
3. Batalin, M., Sukhatme, G.: Spreading out: a local approach to multi-robot coverage. In: Asama, H., Arai, T., Fukuda, T., Hasegawa, T. (eds.) Distributed Autonomous Robotic Systems 5, pp. 373–382. Springer, Heidelberg (2002)
4. Bokareva, T., Bulusu, N., Sanjay, J.: SASHA: toward a self-healing hybrid sensor network architecture. In: The 2nd IEEE Workshop on Embedded Networked Sensors, EmNetS-II, pp. 71–78, May 2005
5. Caliskanelli, I., Harbin, J., Indrusiak, L. Polack, F., Mitchell, P., Chesmore, D.: Runtime optimisation in WSNs for load balancing using pheromone signalling. In: 3rd IEEE International Conference on NESEA, December 2012
6. Caliskanelli, I., Indrusiak, L.: Using mobile robotic agents to increase service availability and extend network lifetime on wireless sensor and robot networks. In: 12th IEEE International Conference on INDIN, July 2014
7. Caliskanelli, I., Harbin, J., Soares Indrusiak, L., Mitchell, P., Polack, F., Chesmore, D.: Bio-inspired load balancing in large-scale wsns using pheromone signalling. Int. J. Distrib. Sens. Netw. **2013**, Article ID 172012, 14 pages (2013)
8. Correll, N., Martinoli, A.: Collective inspection of regular structures using a swarm of miniature robots. In: Ang Jr, M.H., Khatib, O. (eds.) Experimental Robotics IX. Springer Tracts in Advanced Robotics, vol. 21, pp. 375–386. Springer, Heidelberg (2006)
9. Di Caro, G., Dorigo, M.: Antnet: distributed stigmergetic control for communications networks. J. Artif. Int. Res. **9**(1), 317–365 (1998)
10. El-Sherbeny, N.A.: Vehicle routing with time windows: an overview of exact, heuristic and metaheuristic methods. J. King Saud Univ. Sci. **22**(3), 123–131 (2010)
11. Gabriely, Y., Rimon, E.: Spanning-tree based coverage of continuous areas by a mobile robot. Ann. Math. Artif. Intell. **31**(1–4), 77–98 (2001)
12. Gabriely, Y., Rimon, E.: Competitive on-line coverage of grid environments by a mobile robot. Comput. Geom. **24**(3), 197–224 (2003)
13. Gage, D.W.: Command control for many-robot systems. Naval Command Control and Ocean Surveillance Center RDT and E Div San Diego Ca (1992)
14. Gouda, M.G., McGuire, T.M.: Accelerated heartbeat protocols. In: 18th International Conference on Distributed Computing Systems, pp. 202–209 (1998)
15. Gunes, M., Sorges, U., Bouazizi, I.: ARA-the ant-colony based routing algorithm for MANETs. In: Proceedings of the International Conference on Parallel Processing Workshops, pp. 79–85 (2002)

16. Hamouda, Y., Phillips, C.: Biological task mapping and scheduling in wireless sensor networks. In: IEEE International Conference on Communications Technology and Applications, ICCTA 2009, pp. 914–919, October 2009
17. Hazon, N., Kaminka, G.A.: On redundancy, efficiency, and robustness in coverage for multiple robots. Rob. Auton. Syst. **56**(12), 1102–1114 (2008). Towards Autonomous Robotic Systems 2008: Mobile Robotics in the UK 10th British Conference on Mobile Robotics - Towards Autonomous Robotic Systems (TAROS 2007)
18. Heinzelman, W., Chandrakasan, A., Balakrishnan, H.: Energy-efficient communication protocol for wireless microsensor networks. In: Proceedings of the 33rd Annual Hawaii International Conference on System Sciences, vol. 2, p. 10, January 2000
19. Jung, B., Sukhatme, G.: Tracking targets using multiple robots: the effect of environment occlusion. Auton. Rob. **13**(3), 191–205 (2002)
20. Karaboga, D., Basturk, B.: On the performance of artificial bee colony (ABC) algorithm. Appl. Soft Comput. **8**(1), 687–697 (2008)
21. Karaboga, D.: Artificial bee colony algorithm. Scholarpedia **5**(3), 6915 (2010)
22. Khatib, O.: Real-time obstacle avoidance for manipulators and mobile robots. In: Proceedings of the 1985 IEEE International Conference on Robotics and Automation, vol. 2, pp. 500–505, March 1985
23. Kloder, S.: Barrier Coverage: Deploying Robot Guards to Prevent Intrusion. ProQuest, Ann Arbor (2008)
24. Lemmens, N., de Jong, S., Tuyls, K., Nowé, A.: Bee behaviour in multi-agent systems. In: Tuyls, K., Nowe, A., Guessoum, Z., Kudenko, D. (eds.) Adaptive Agents and MAS III. LNCS (LNAI), vol. 4865, pp. 145–156. Springer, Heidelberg (2008)
25. Packer, E.: Robust geometric computing and optimal visibility coverage. Ph.D. thesis, Stony Brook, NY, USA (2008). aAI3338238
26. Pirzadeh, A., Snyder, W.: A unified solution to coverage and search in explored and unexplored terrains using indirect control. In: Proceedings of the 1990 IEEE International Conference on Robotics and Automation, vol. 3, pp. 2113–2119, May 1990
27. Ranjbar-Sahraei, B., Weiss, G., Nakisaee, A.: Stigmergic coverage algorithm for multi-robot systems (demonstration). In: Proceedings of the 11th International Conference AAMAS, vol. 3, pp. 1497–1498 (2012)
28. Roberts, M.B.V.: Biology: A Functional Approach. Nelson, Surrey (1986). http://www.worldcat.org/isbn/0174480199
29. Sahoo, R.R., Sardar, A.R., Singh, M., Ray, S., Sarkar, S.K.: Trust based secure and energy efficient clustering in wireless sensor network: a bee mating approach. In: Maji, P., Ghosh, A., Murty, M.N., Ghosh, K., Pal, S.K. (eds.) PReMI 2013. LNCS, vol. 8251, pp. 100–107. Springer, Heidelberg (2013)
30. Sahraei, B.R., Alers, S., Tuyls, K., Weiss, G.: Stico in action. In: International Conference on Autonomous Agents and Multi-Agent Systems, AAMAS 2013, Saint Paul, MN, USA, pp. 1403–1404, 6–10 May 2013
31. Saleem, M., Farooq, M.: BeeSensor: a bee-inspired power aware routing protocol for wireless sensor networks. In: Giacobini, M. (ed.) EvoWorkshops 2007. LNCS, vol. 4448, pp. 81–90. Springer, Heidelberg (2007)
32. Sarafijanovic, S., Le Boudec, J.Y.: An artificial immune system approach with secondary response for misbehavior detection in mobile ad hoc networks. IEEE Trans. Neural Netw. **16**(5), 1076–1087 (2005)

33. Sarafijanović, S., Le Boudec, J.-Y.: An artificial immune system for misbehavior detection in mobile ad-hoc networks with virtual thymus, clustering, danger signal, and memory detectors. In: Nicosia, G., Cutello, V., Bentley, P.J., Timmis, J. (eds.) ICARIS 2004. LNCS, vol. 3239, pp. 342–356. Springer, Heidelberg (2004)
34. Senthilkumar, J., Chandrasekaran, M.: Improving the performance of wireless sensor network using bee's mating intelligence. European Journal of Scientific Research **55**(3), 452 (2011)
35. Sheng, W., Yang, Q., Tan, J., Xi, N.: Distributed multi-robot coordination in area exploration. Rob. Auton. Syst. **54**(12), 945–955 (2006)
36. Wedde, H.F., Farooq, M., Zhang, Y.: BeeHive: an efficient fault-tolerant routing algorithm inspired by Honey bee behavior. In: Dorigo, M., Birattari, M., Blum, C., Gambardella, L.M., Mondada, F., Stützle, T. (eds.) ANTS 2004. LNCS, vol. 3172, pp. 83–94. Springer, Heidelberg (2004)
37. Hu, X.-M., Zhang, J.: Ant routing optimization algorithm for extending the lifetime of wireless sensor networks. In: 2010 IEEE International Conference on SMC, pp. 738–744, October 2010
38. Zlot, R., Stentz, A., Dias, M.B., Thayer, S.: Multi-robot exploration controlled by a market economy. In: ICRA, pp. 3016–3023. IEEE (2002)

Author Index

Printed in the United States
By Bookmasters

Printed in the United States
By Bookmasters